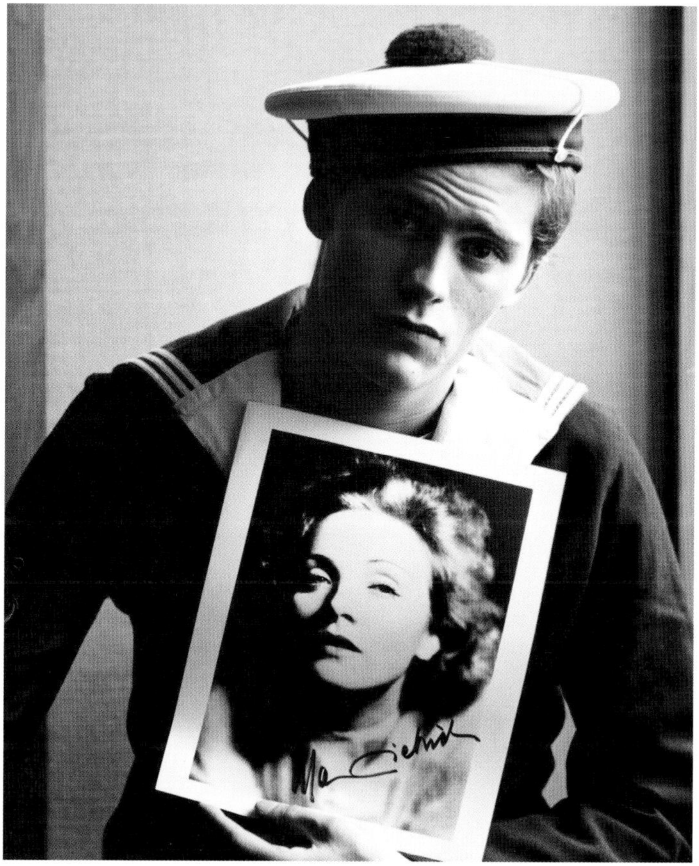

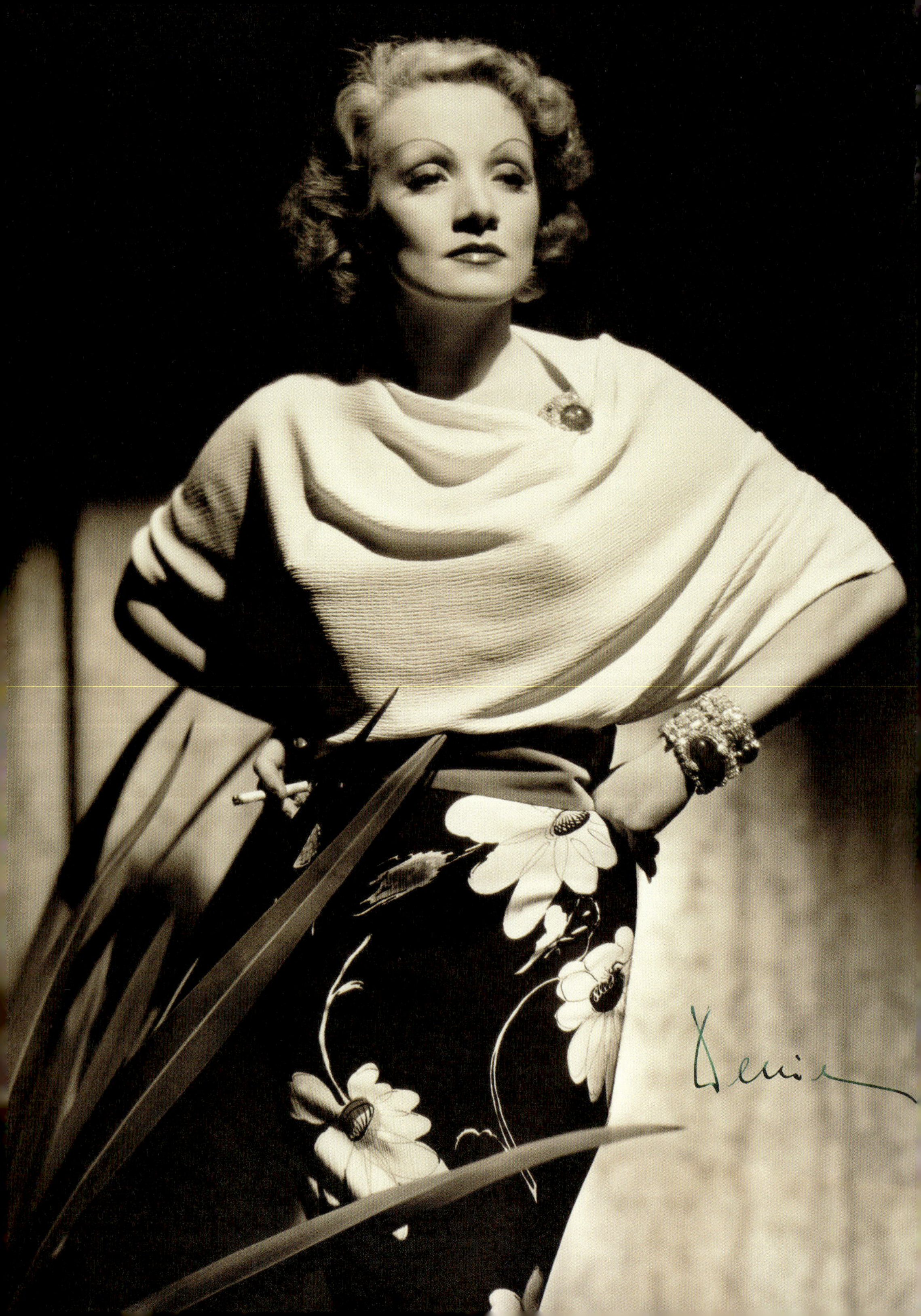

Henry-Jean Servat

OBSESSION MARLENE DIETRICH

The Pierre Passebon Collection

Flammarion

EDITORIAL DIRECTOR
Suzanne Tise-Isoré
Style & Design Collection

EDITORIAL COORDINATION
Gwendoline Blanchard

GRAPHIC DESIGN
Bernard Lagacé
and Lysandre Le Cléa'ch

ICONOGRAPHER
Marie-Nicole Féret

TRANSLATED FROM THE FRENCH
Barbara Mellor

CAPTIONS
Mark Vieira

COPYEDITING AND PROOFREADING
Lindsay Porter

PRODUCTION
Marie-Hélène Lafin

COLOR SEPARATION
Les Artisans du Regard

PRINTED BY
Stamperia artistica

Simultaneously published in French as
Obsession Marlene : la collection Pierre Passebon

English-language edition

Flammarion S.A.
87, quai Panhard et Levassor
75647 Paris Cedex 13
editions.flammarion.com
styleetdesign-flammarion.com

ISBN: 978-2-08-020357-1
Editorial number: L.01EBTN000825
Legal deposit: November 2017
Printed in Italy

Page 1
PATRICE CALMETTES, c. 1980

Photographer Calmettes was Marlene's friend and confidant.

Page 2
EUGENE ROBERT RICHEE (Supervised by Josef von Sternberg), 1936

Richee was an accomplished portraitist, but Dietrich insisted
that Sternberg continue to supervise her photographs, even though
he was no longer directing her.

Facing page
EDWARD STEICHEN, 1935

Steichen has been called America's greatest photographer.
He made this portrait of Dietrich on March 26, 1935,
and it ran in the June 1 issue of *Vanity Fair*.

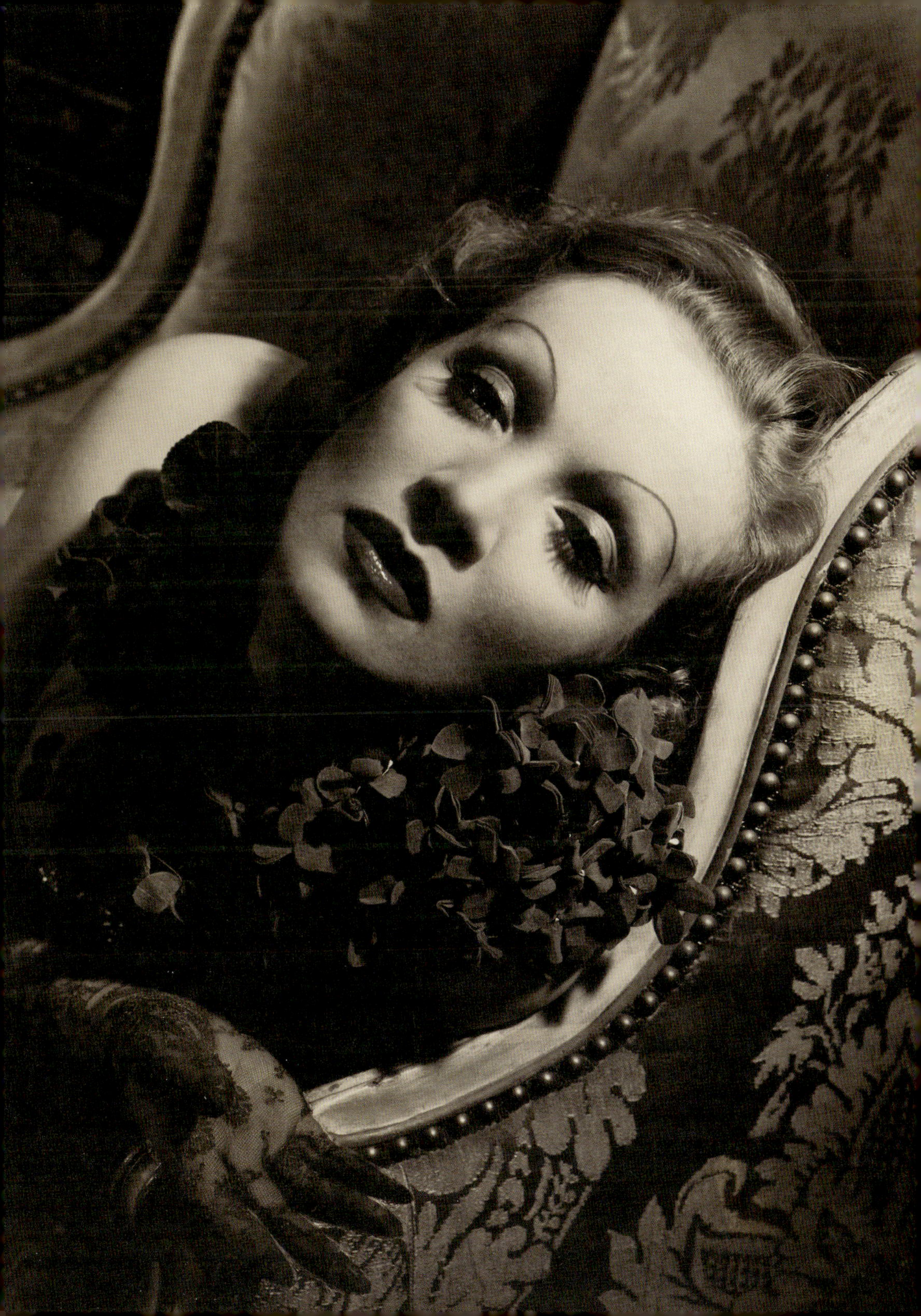

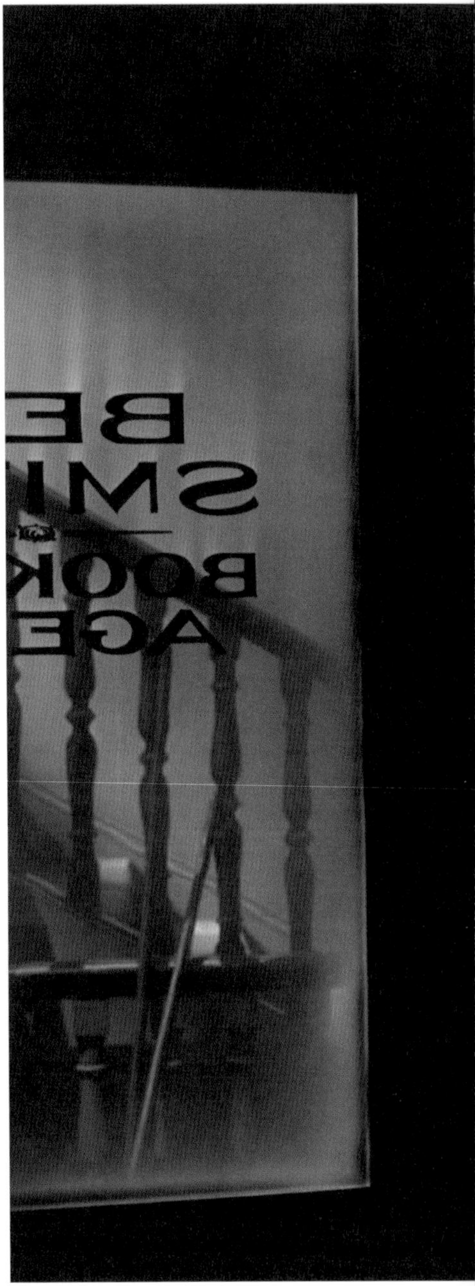

DON ENGLISH (Supervised by Josef von Sternberg), 1932

This posed production still from *Blonde Venus* shows Sternberg directing Dietrich. His superb cinematography illuminated Marlene on seven movies, from 1930 to 1935. At the time, Hollywood studios preferred posed shots to candid shots, because they could be carefully lit, composed, and retouched.

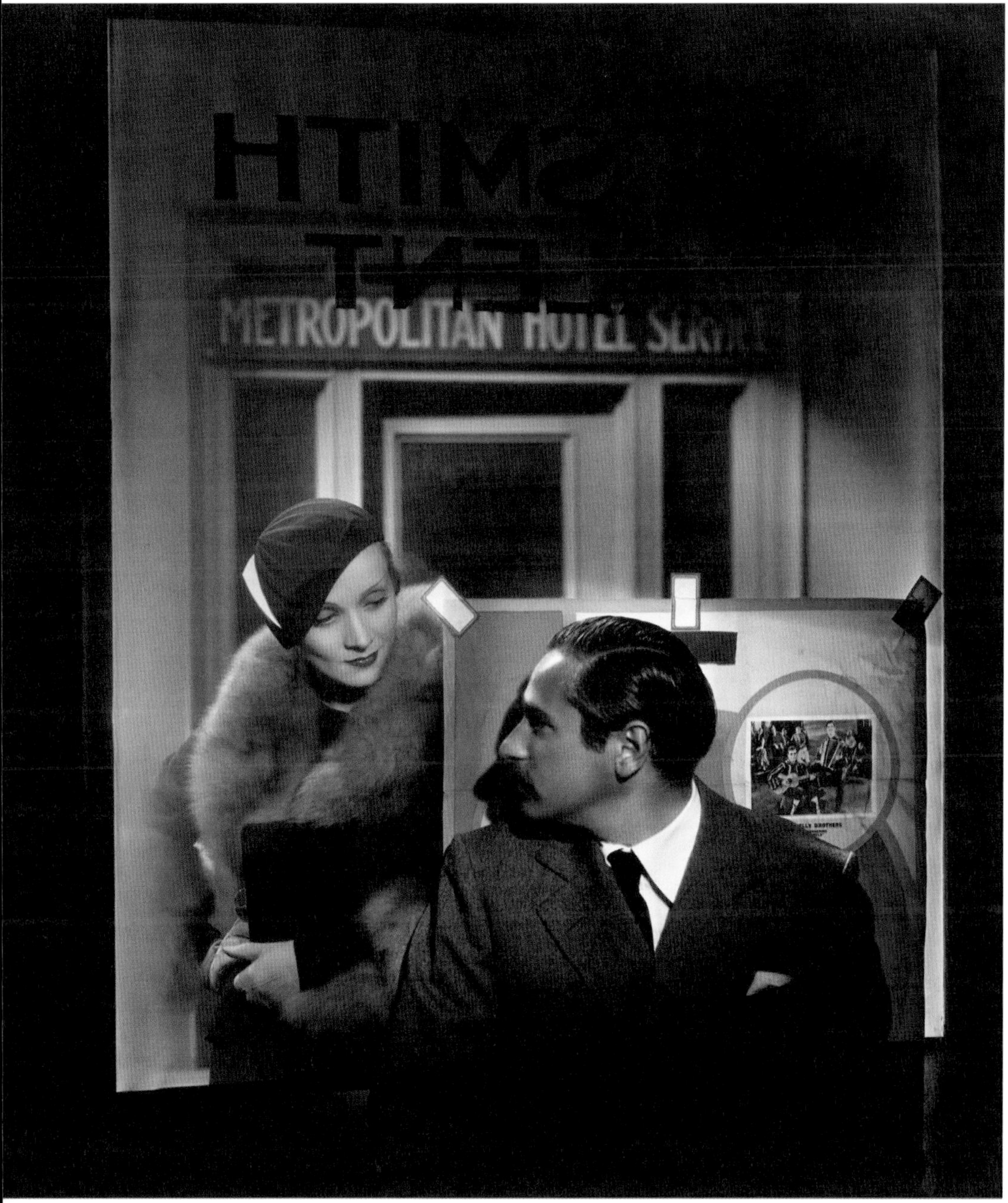
METROPOLITAN HOTEL

HENRY-JEAN SERVAT

Interview with Pierre Passebon

HENRI-JEAN SERVAT "Obsession"—as in the title of the book—is a strong word, really strong. This is the title you have chosen for your fascinating collection.

PIERRE PASSEBON Yes, but it tells the truth, it's the *mot juste*. It is the word that best defines my feelings for Marlene Dietrich. What I feel for her, what I have always felt for her, is a genuine obsession. I am obsessed by her life, by the things she did, by her style, by the images we have of her, and by her image. And it goes back a long time—long before I started my photographic collection.

HJS When you speak of Dietrich, you are obviously referring to her as a person, as a persona, and as a personality. What was it about her that led you to become obsessed with her in the first place?

PP I sensed straight away that she was someone I might have as a friend, someone who might be part of my inner circle, someone to love and admire, who would be at once close and aloof. From the moment I first set eyes on her in the cinema, I saw her as someone who was profoundly modern.

HJS Did you ever meet her, or even catch a glimpse of her?

PP No, never. And that's why I am obsessed with her and why I pursue her around the globe. I hunt out photographs of her, I track them down, and acquire them for my collection. I have over two thousand of them.

IRVING CHIDNOFF, 1933

Dietrich's first American publicity photo was shot when she arrived in New York in May 1930. Chidnoff was a respected society and theater portraitist who worked in the soft, flat style of the period.

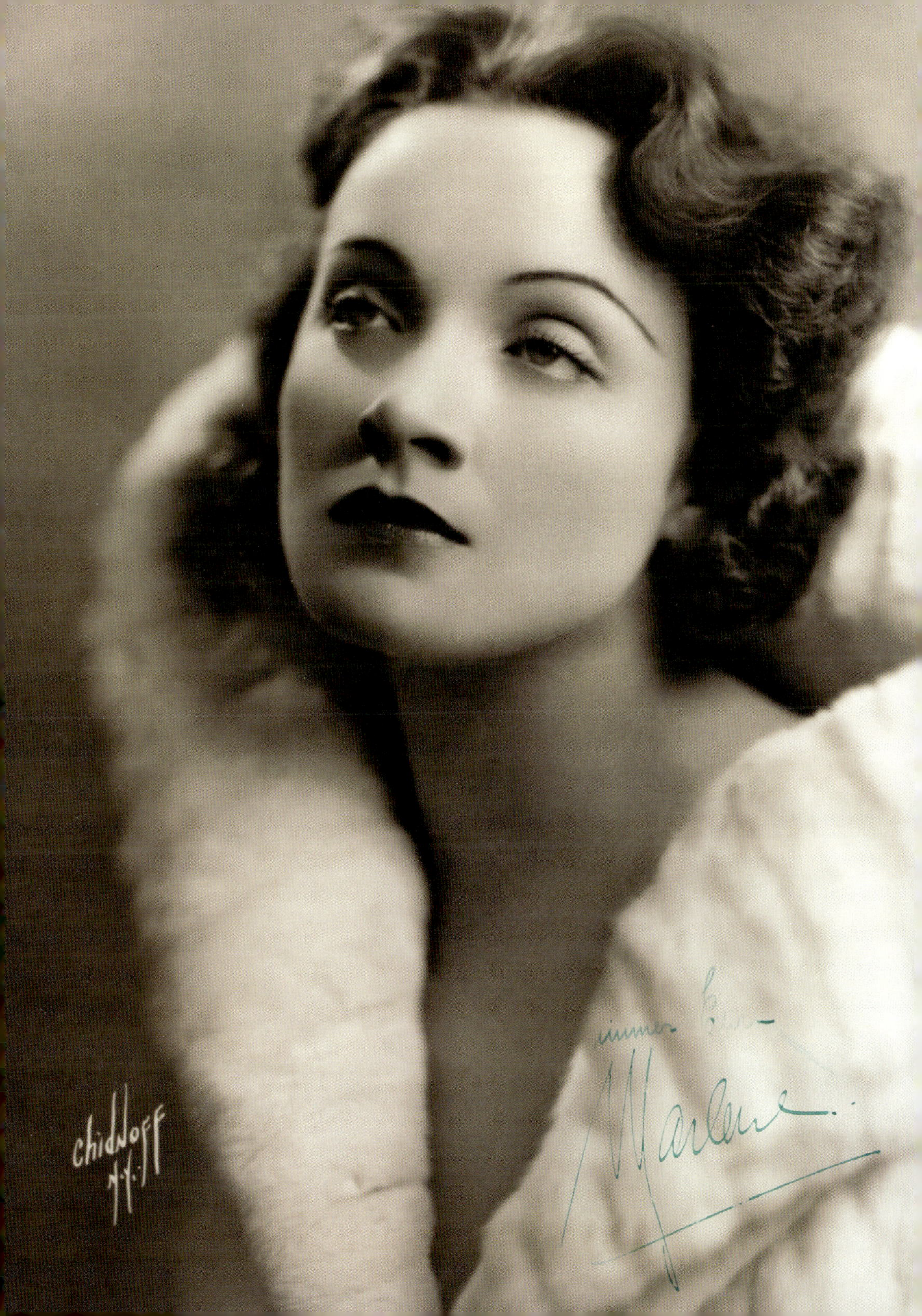

Chidnoff
N.Y.
Marlene

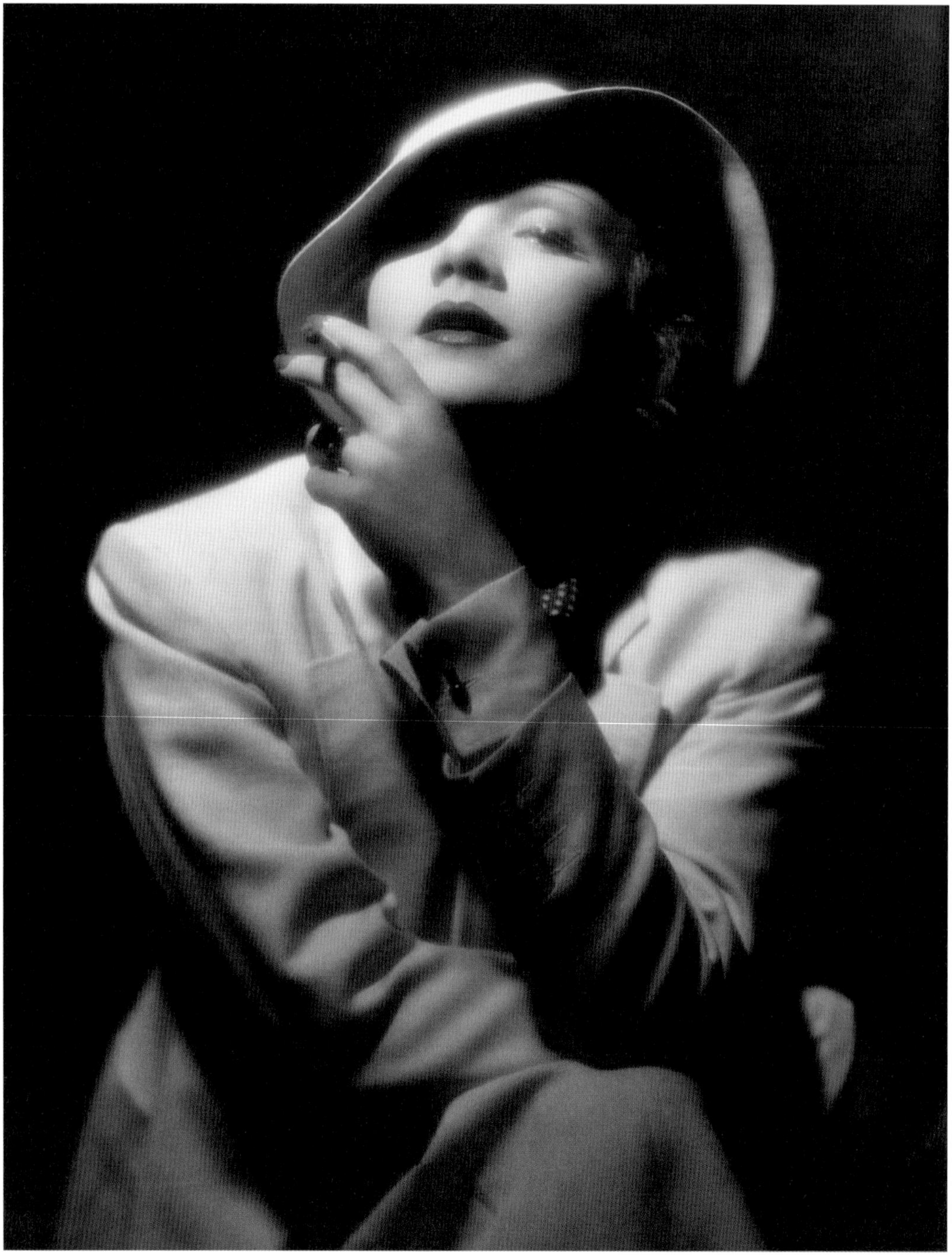

HJS You view her as completely modern today? Yet the image that we have of her is enshrined in films of the 1930s, '40s, and '50s. In other words in vintage settings, yellowed by time.

PP I think her films are magnificent thanks to her presence, which is so different, so unconventional. Her personality can't be contained, it spills out of them. There is nothing anodyne or ordinary about them. And they exist, like jewel boxes, as a setting for the gem that is Dietrich. Her films and photographs shaped and established her fame, ensuring her a place in and for eternity. They can seem formidable, and make her appear more aloof; we are held at a distance, transfixed by our feelings of respect and veneration. In fact, it was the way she chose to live that made her far more approachable, more profoundly moving. We shouldn't forget that from 1953 and right up to 1974 she gave concerts and cabaret performances that made her magnetic presence even more accessible to the public. Her voice drew as much admiration as her legs.

HJS How is it that Dietrich—the person, persona, and personality, the eternal presence and legendary actress—can appear today as radically modern?

PP Dietrich's modernity resides, I really believe, in the way she chose to live and to lead her career. She was a liberated woman, tolerant, ethical, and deeply humane. She was not arrogant. Her generosity was legendary.

WILLIAM WALLING, JR. (Supervised by Josef von Sternberg), 1932

Dietrich and Sternberg did some of their best portrait work in collaboration with William Walling, Jr., who had left a career in acting to become a photographer.

HJS You say that her image is modern. By "image" we understand her look, her style. So her modernity is channeled by the images we have of her, by her sense of style in the way she dressed, her involvement in the world of fashion, and the graphic quality of her silhouette.

PP Dietrich's conception of her body was always highly graphic, both in space and in time. Of all the actresses of her generation, she remains the one who devoted herself most completely and successfully to this graphic conception of her physical presence. She knew better than anyone how to project her silhouette, how to occupy the limelight.

HJS It came more easily to her than to others. She had the spirit and determination of an architect, constructing herself out of fabrics and dreams. All the couturiers and costume designers with whom she worked were her friends.

PP Yes, of course, but she had her likes and dislikes. She adored Madame Grès, for example, who was her friend like many others. When she went to be dressed by Chanel, on the other hand, she would flatly refuse to see Coco Chanel because of the way she behaved with the Germans during World War II. Dietrich would not forgive her for it, and there was no question of meeting her, even at home. She was absolutely clear about this.

HJS Did she get involved in haute couture in Hollywood?

PP Actresses in the golden age of the Hollywood studios would be "dressed"—let's say they were happy to be dressed without getting involved in the design of their on-screen wardrobes. Costume designers employed by the studios would design their outfits and tell them what to wear, when, and how. The actresses went along with this, and the results were often magnificent.

EUGENE ROBERT RICHEE (Supervised by Josef von Sternberg), 1930

In Dietrich's first American film, *Morocco*, she played a cabaret singer whose apartment is full of portraits of herself. This pose was intended as one of those portraits, but it also became a widely seen image.

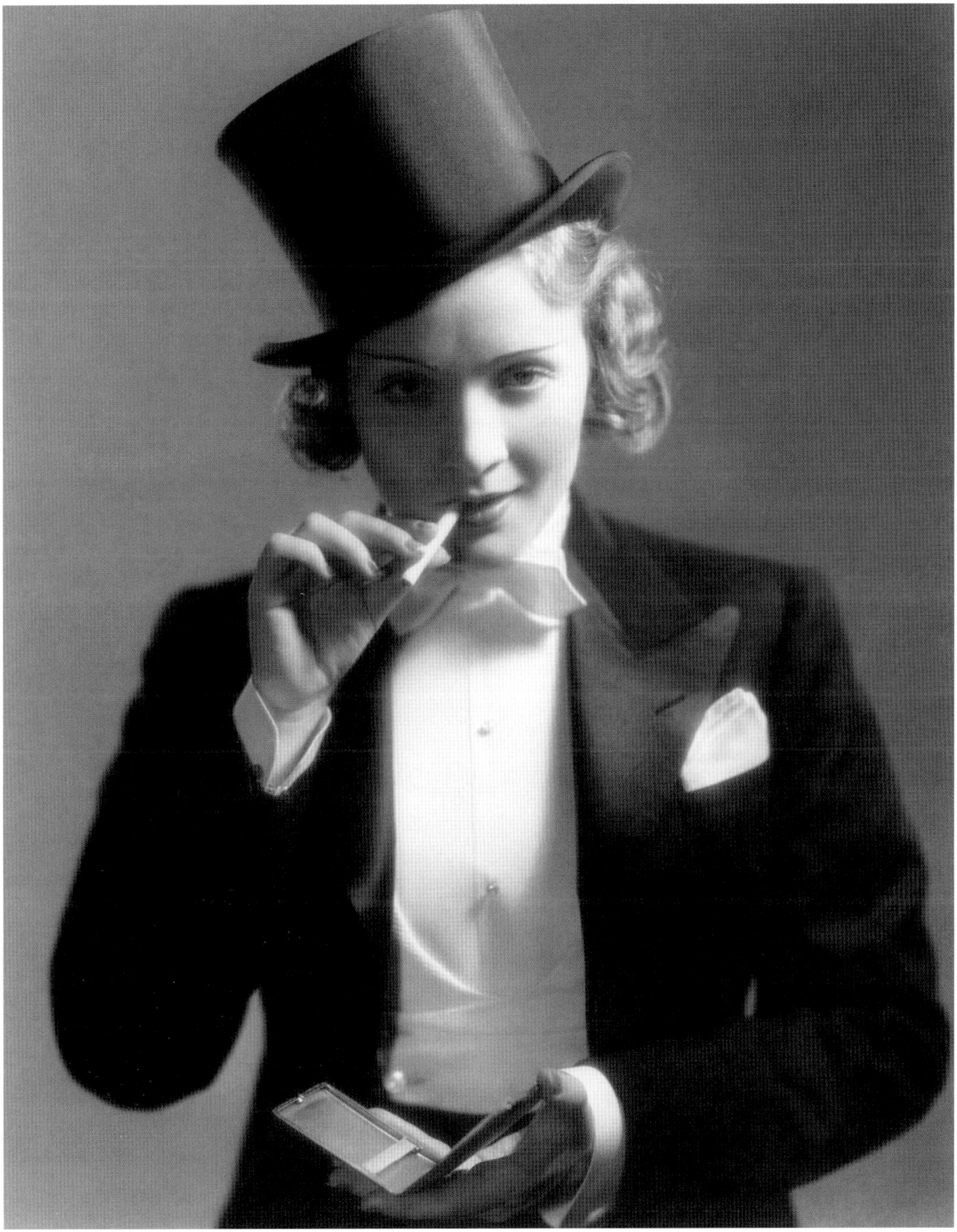

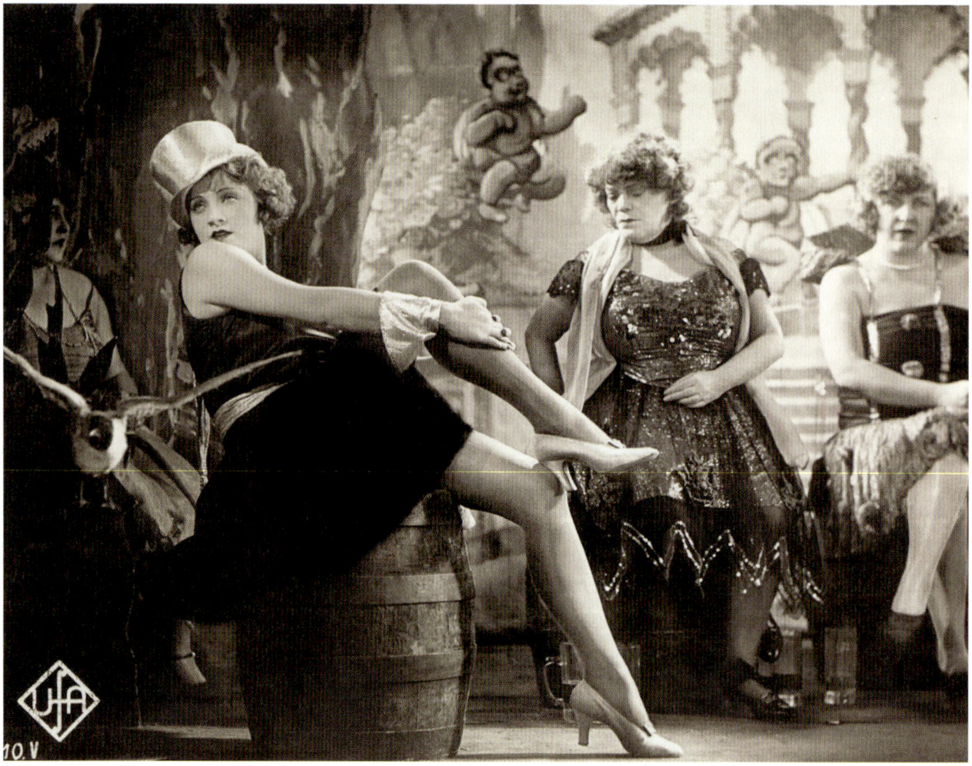

MARIO VON BUKOVICH (Supervised by Josef von Sternberg), 1929

The Blue Angel was Germany's first all-talking film and Dietrich's first film with Sternberg. Although she had been working in German film for six years, she was publicized as an "overnight" sensation. On the right, the photograph before censorship. It's very rare to find both versions and to be able to compare them like this.

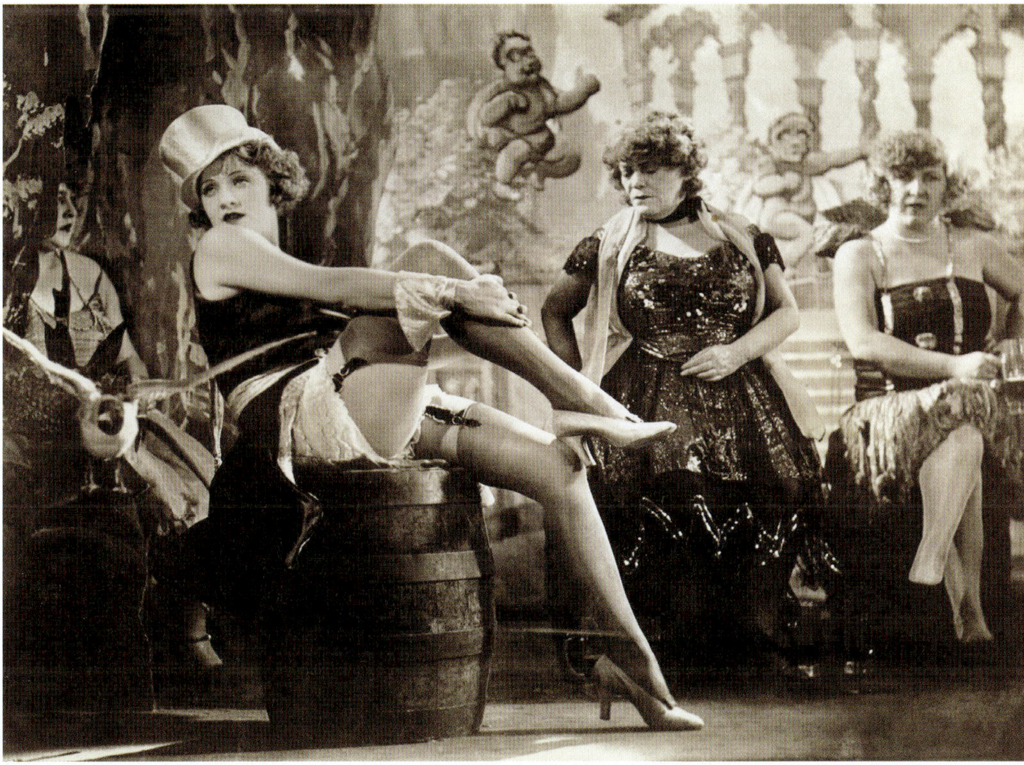

"We know God made trees
And the birds and the bees
And seas for the fishes to swim in
We are also aware,
That he had quite a flair
For creating exceptional women.
[...]
Now we all might enjoy
Seeing Helen of Troy
As a gay cabaret entertainer.
But I doubt that she could
Be one quarter as good
As our legendary, lovely
Marlene."

MARLENE, NOEL COWARD, 1954

DON ENGLISH (Supervised by Josef von Sternberg), 1932

Cinematographer Lee Garmes won an Academy Award for his work on *Shanghai Express*. This scene was lit by him, so Sternberg instructed English to capture the setup, and then to create variations of it. It was used as a poster for the Cannes Film Festival in 1992, the year of Marlene's death.

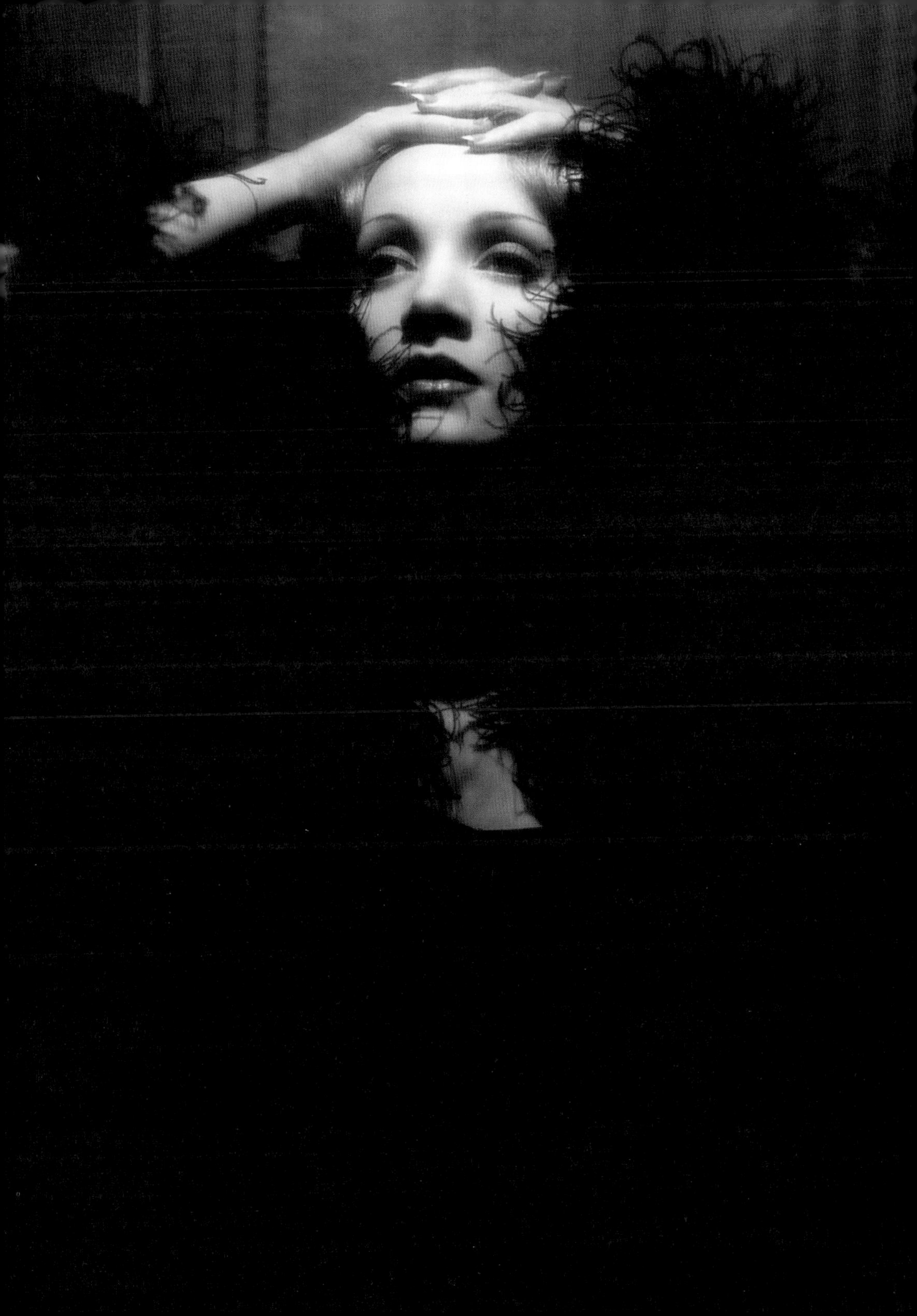

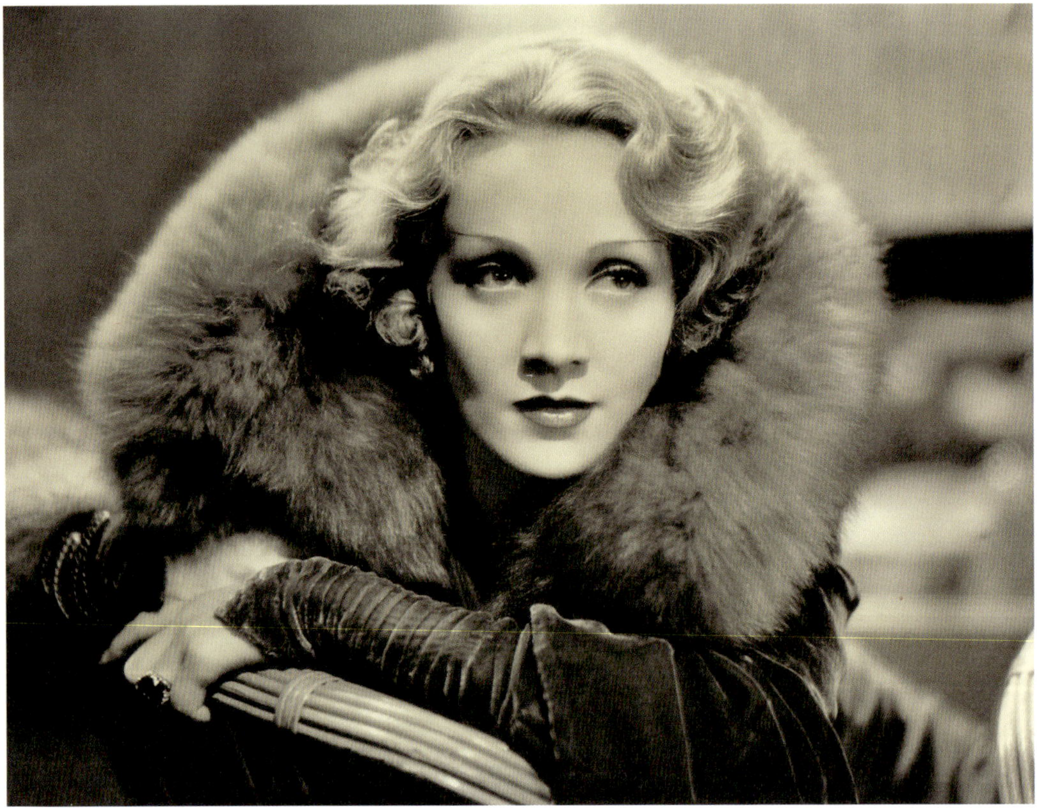

DON ENGLISH (Supervised by Josef von Sternberg), 1932

After the director said "Cut!" it was time for the unit still photographer to say, "Hold for stills!". Sternberg often instructed the photographer to stylize the scene still into a portrait, as in this *Shanghai Express* pose.

WILLIAM WALLING, JR. (Supervised by Josef von Sternberg), 1933

In this session, Sternberg had Dietrich wear costumes that had feathers affixed to them, playing up the image of a bird.

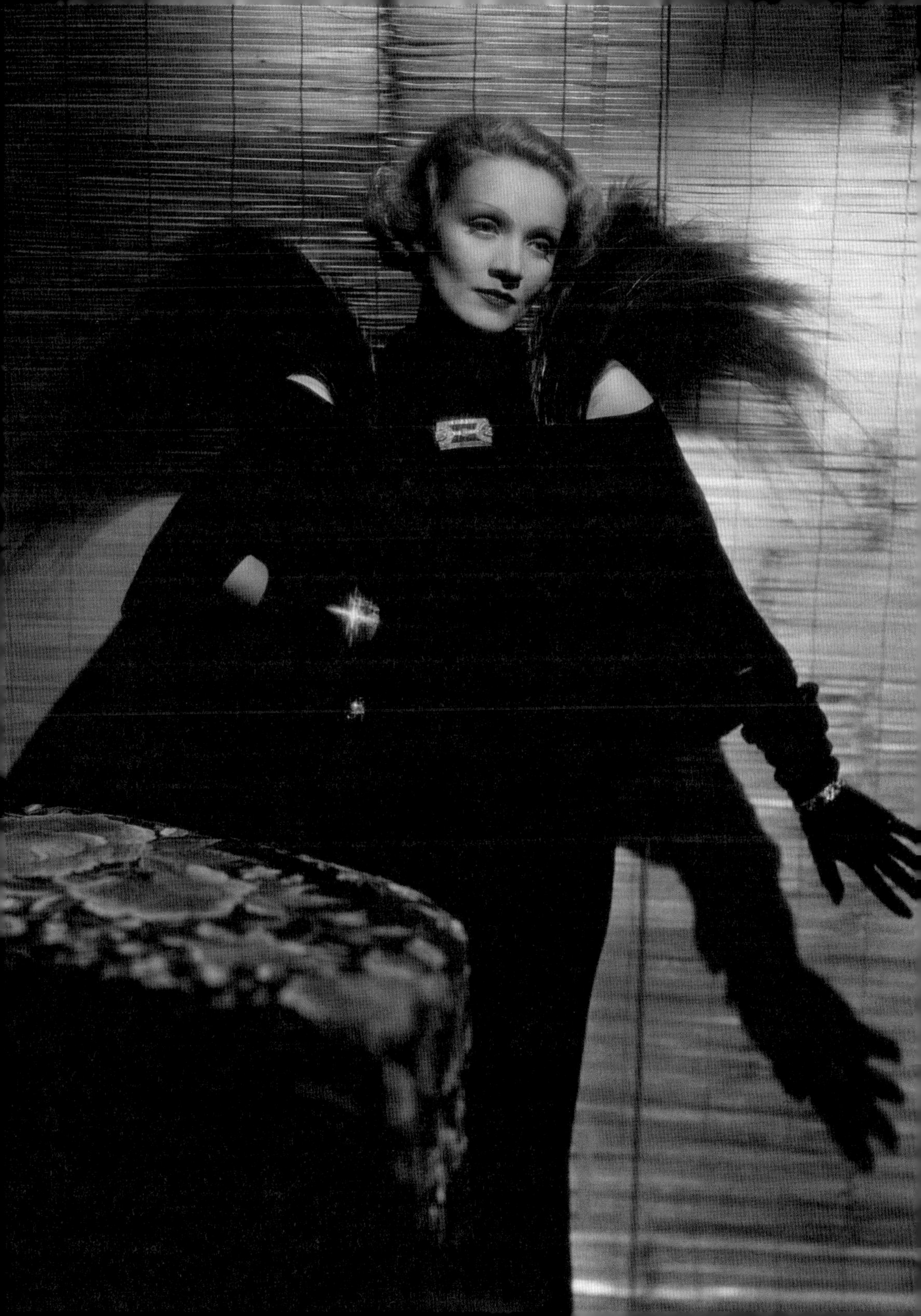

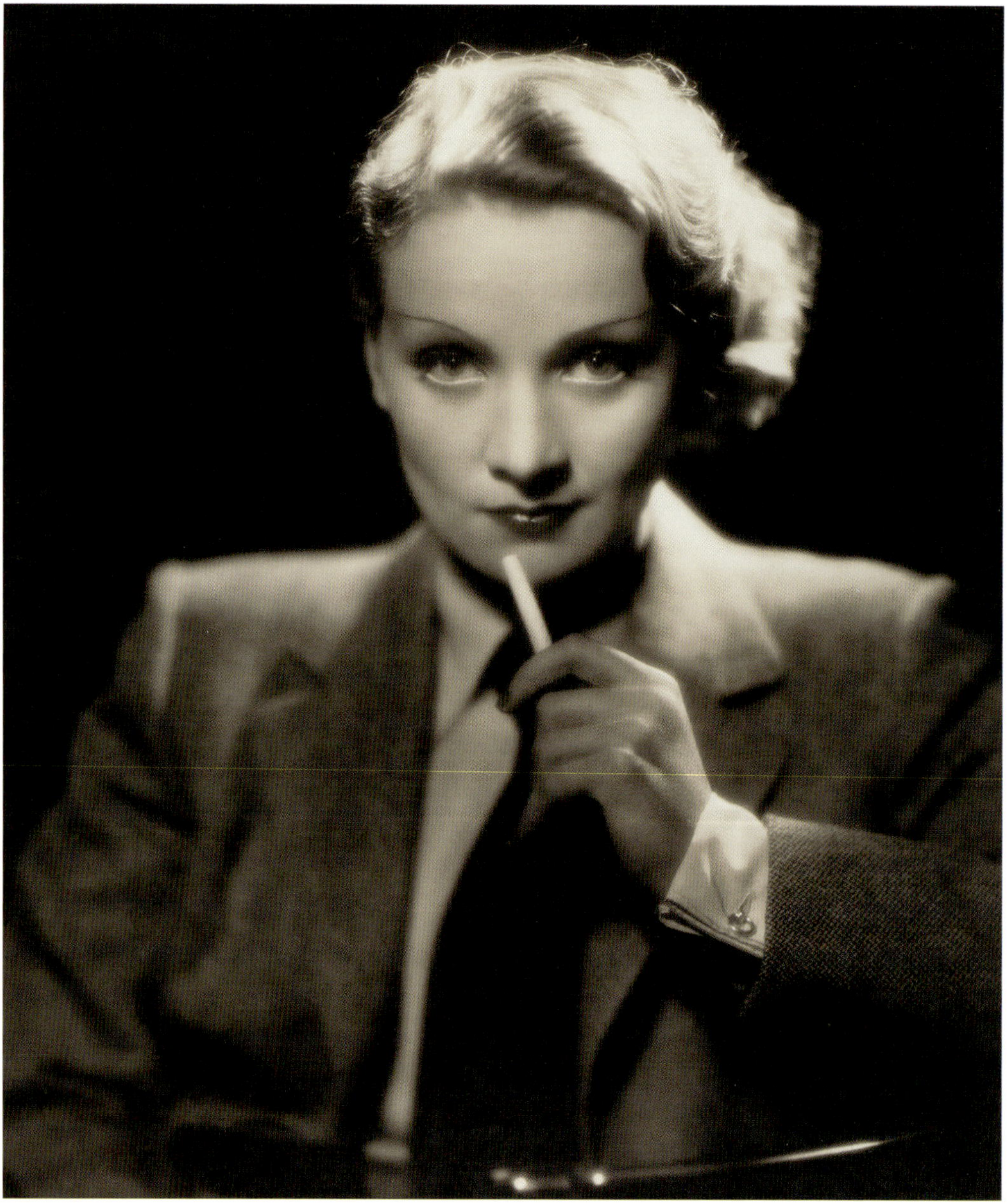

WILLIAM WALLING, JR. (Supervised by Josef von Sternberg), 1932

Dietrich had achieved fame in her first American films for wearing men's clothes, a habit she carried into her offscreen life. Sternberg capitalized on this in a series of evocative soft-focus portraits.

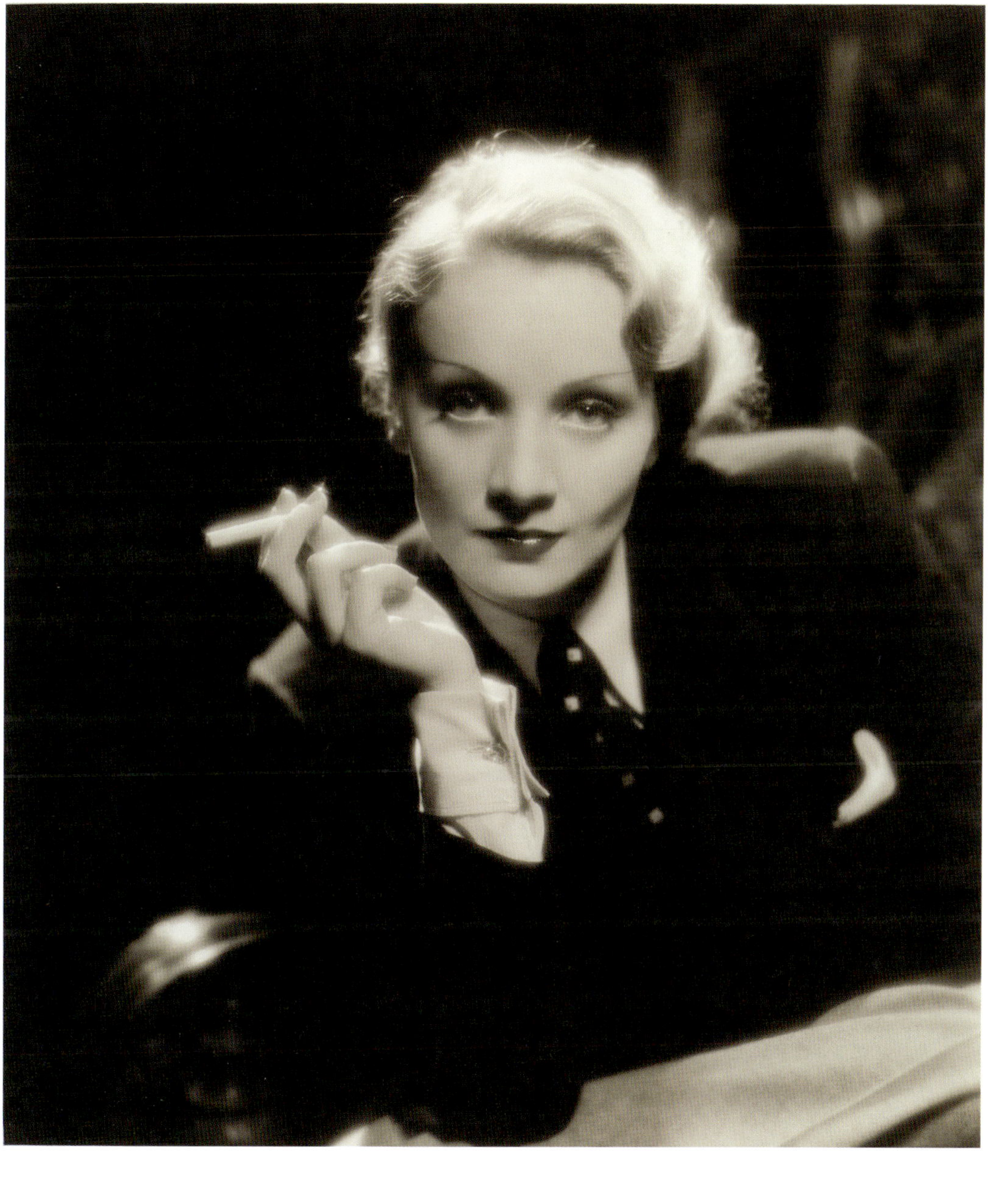

WILLIAM WALLING, JR. (Supervised by Josef von Sternberg), 1932

In the worst year of the Great Depression, images of Dietrich helped young people to escape stress and aspire to success. Her ever-present cigarette also influenced young Americans with her gesture of effortless allure.

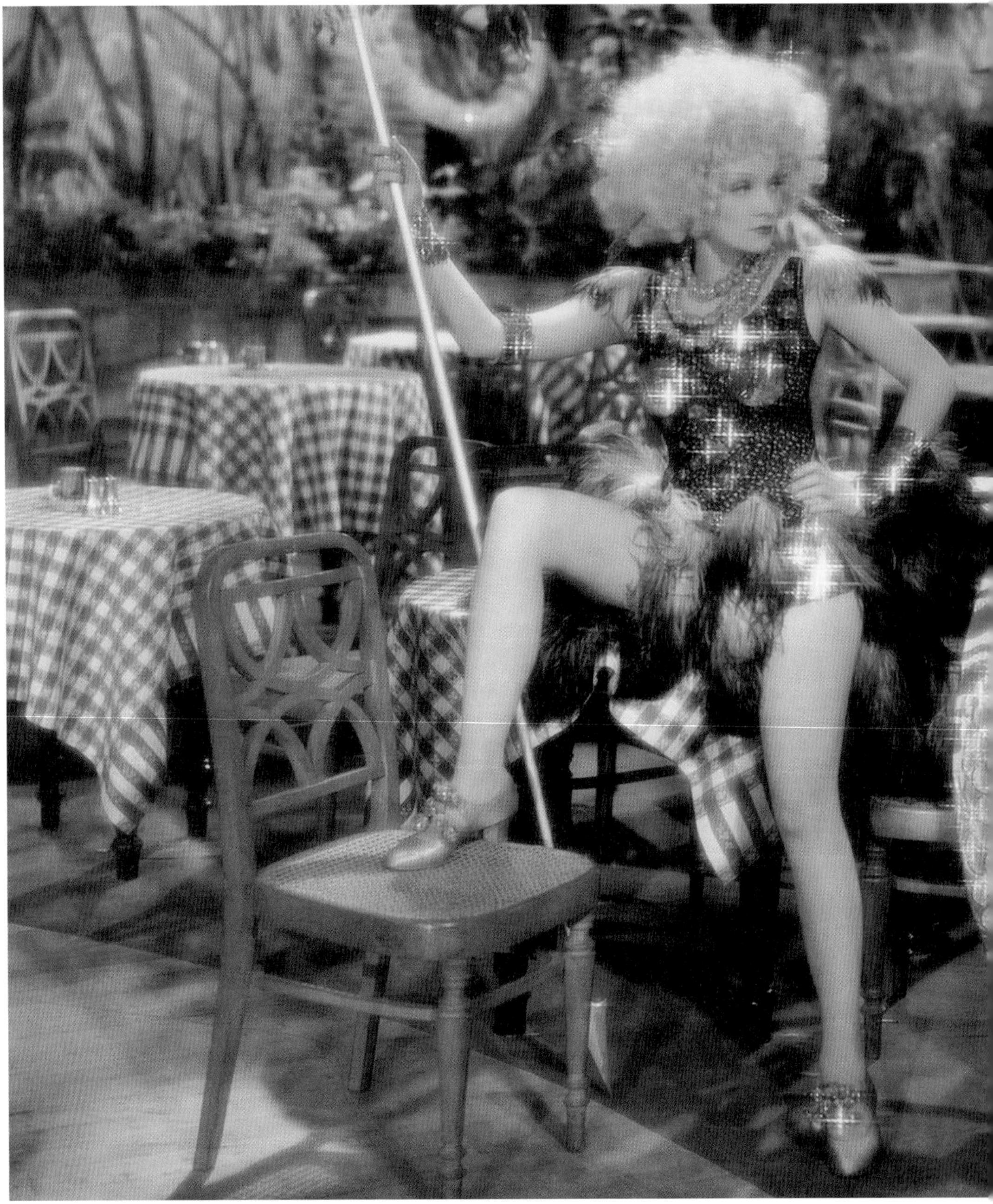

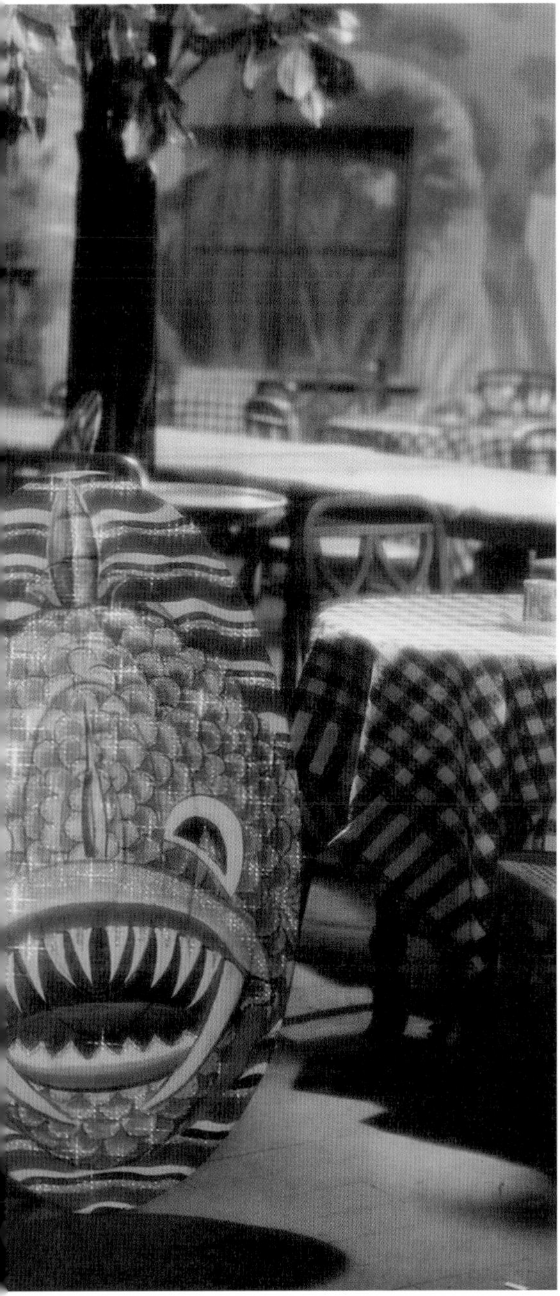

DON ENGLISH (Supervised by Josef von Sternberg), 1932

This on-set portrait was made by the unit still photographer for *Blonde Venus*, the fifth of the seven films Dietrich made with Sternberg. She is posed in a nightclub set for the musical number "Hot Voodoo," one of her best and most spectacular acts.

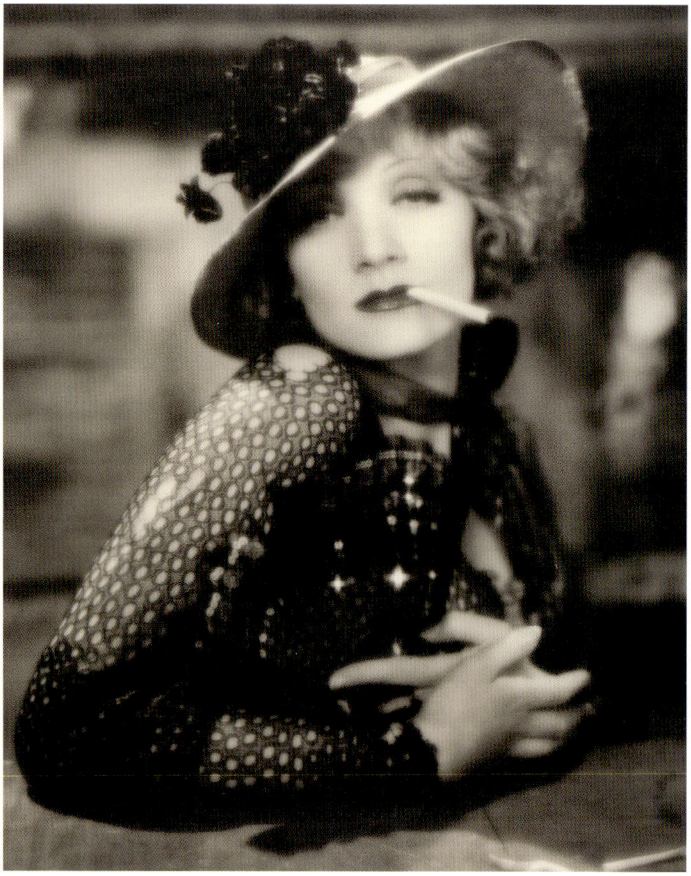

DON ENGLISH (Supervised by Josef von Sternberg), 1932

In *Blonde Venus*, Dietrich plays a devoted wife who sells herself to save her husband from a deadly illness. For her troubles, she is chased and hounded until she ends up in a Galveston dive, looking like this.

DON ENGLISH (Supervised by Josef von Sternberg), 1932

Dietrich posed in the *Blonde Venus* dressing-room set for this portrait by English. Only Josef von Sternberg and Cecil B. DeMille allowed their still photographers as much time and latitude between takes.

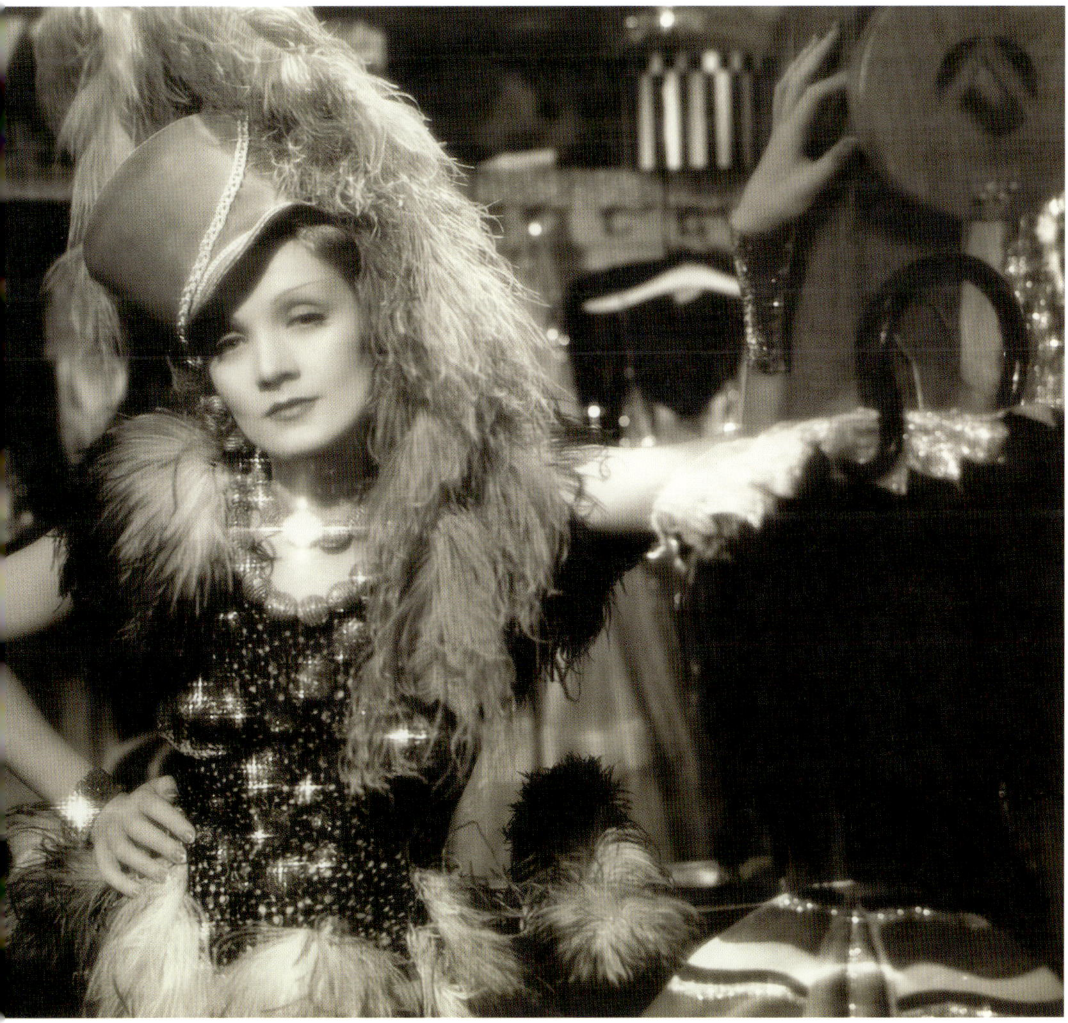

HJS But Dietrich was involved in the design of her wardrobe ...

PP Dietrich had an inspired sense of costume and fashion, combined with a practical sensibility. On one occasion, she even invented a brassiere that was integrated into the dress she was wearing, which increased her freedom of movement. She could dress herself, arrange things for her own convenience, and do rapid costume changes on set. When she wanted to wear a long white coat on her last concert tour, she chose the lightest swansdown for it. No one could have imagined that this imposing garment hung so lightly on her shoulders. And everyone knows about the semi-transparent gowns that she was supposed to have been sewn into for her gala appearances.

HJS She made the decision that she would not wear just anything. She chose her own screen wardrobe and put her own outfits together as she wanted them, and she would never have worn a costume that did not suit her, that she had not approved in every detail, from top to toe. It mattered to her, and it mattered above all for her image.

PP Yes. Dietrich dressed exclusively for her image. She wanted to exist in the way people saw her and in the stunning effect she created. Her daughter, Maria Riva, described how her interest lay far more in the way her characters looked than in their names, which she would often forget, or their lines, which she frequently found witless. She even adopted the scandalous habit pioneered by lesbians of dressing like a man. It was an instant success. But whether she was in top hat and tails or in flamboyant creations of feathers, lace, and pompoms, it was always Dietrich who wore her outfits rather than vice versa; her outfits were always subservient to her, as her photographs bear witness.

SCOTTY WELBOURNE, 1941

In this portrait for *Manpower*, Welbourne uses the lighting scheme seen in portraits made by Sternberg, Richee, and Walling at Paramount.

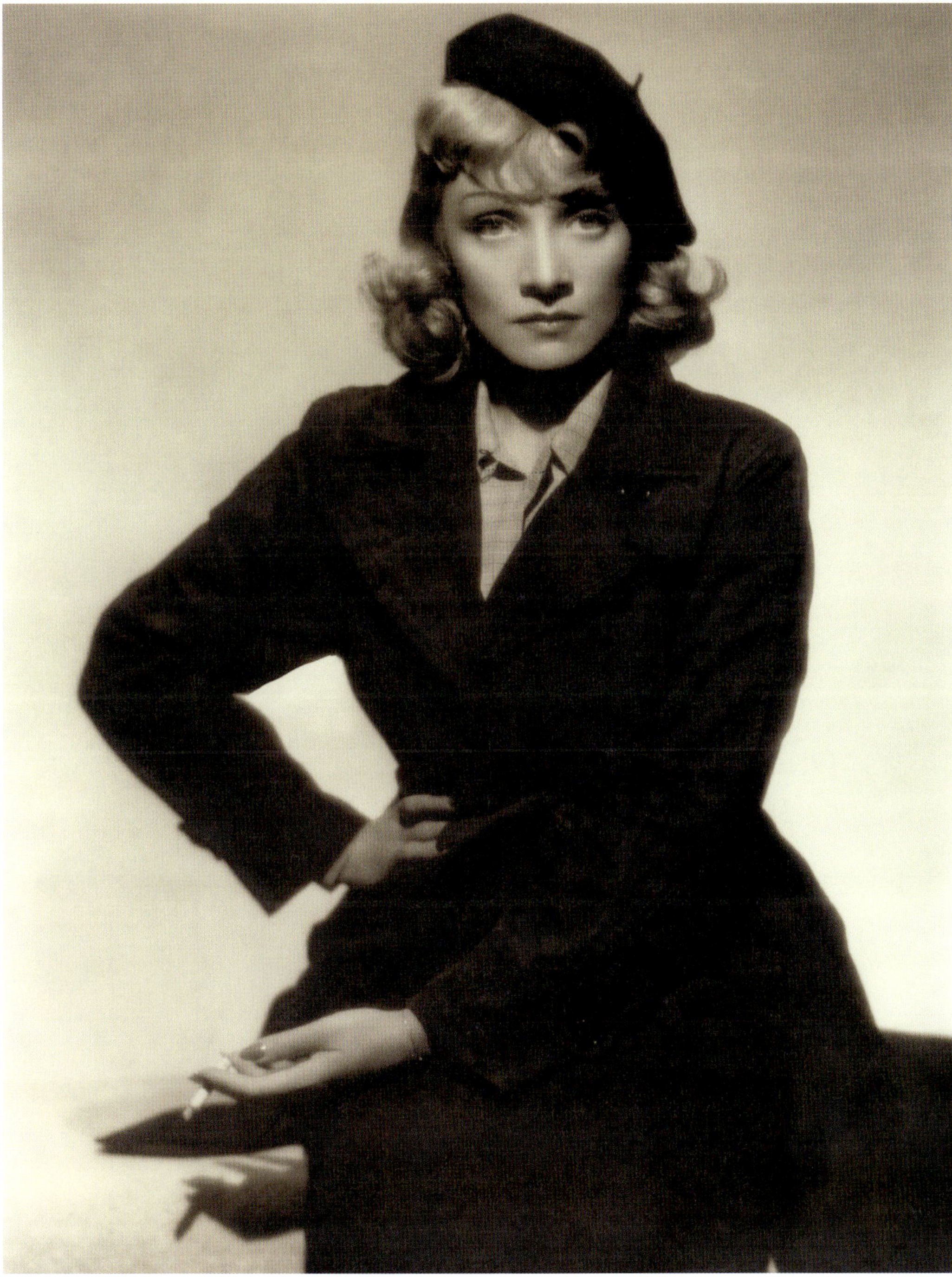

"Dietrich is a study of contrasts in many ways. She was known for her discipline and dedication to her craft while unapologetically breaking social barriers and embracing female independence."

KATE C. LEMAY, CURATOR OF THE SMITHSONIAN'S
NATIONAL PORTRAIT GALLERY EXHIBITION
MARLENE DIETRICH: DRESSED FOR THE IMAGE, 2017–2018.

UNSIGNED PRESS PHOTO, 1933

In 1933 Dietrich sailed on the SS *Europa* to Cherbourg, France. Photographs of her masculine traveling attire were featured in newspapers, newsreels, and movie magazines.

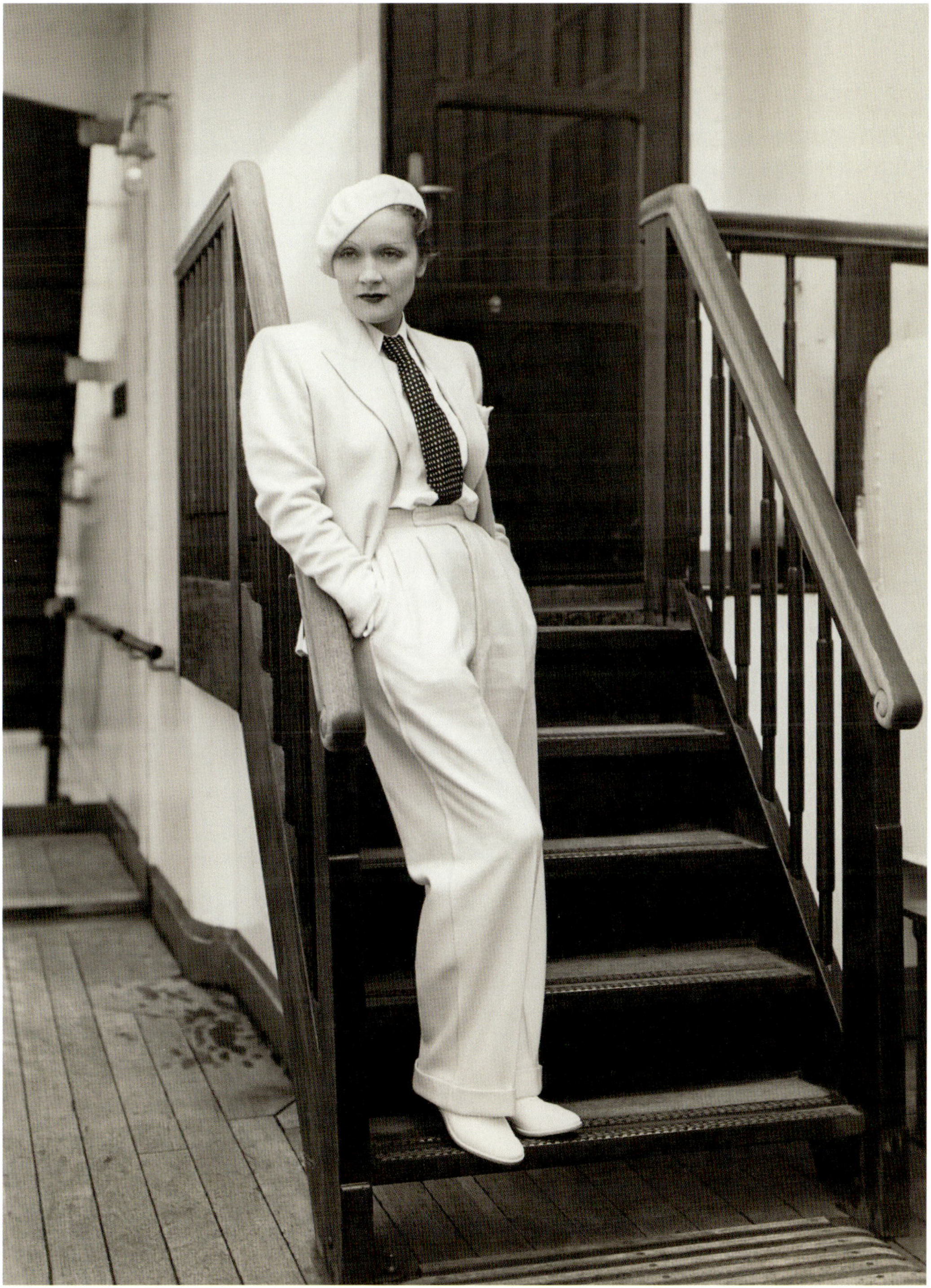

HJS In her films, she very often liked to pose in men's clothes, in fact?

PP The very idea of wearing men's clothes in a feminine way—she was steadfastly a woman—as she did in many of her films, was hers. She invented it, disseminated it, and popularized it. Later it would be taken up by Yves Saint Laurent.

HJS When Saint Laurent designed his men's tuxedo for women, did he know that Dietrich had invented it, long before his time?

PP Yes, he most certainly did. One of Yves Saint Laurent's sources of inspiration was the cinema. Dietrich wore the men's tuxedo after suggesting it to the directors she worked with, and she did so with their blessing. She knew that men's evening attire suited her to perfection. So she played the game, she wore it, and launched a fashion, and the results—invariably impeccable—are a vision of modernity, and a glorious one. Dietrich knew with absolute clarity what suited her to perfection. She had an acute awareness of it.

HJS An awareness, you say?

PP Absolutely. She was acutely aware of what she owed to herself. As she liked to say, "All my life I have represented glamour in a milieu that was anything but glamorous," often adding, "People come not to see me but to look at me."

HJS We should also mention that as well as wearing men's suits, Dietrich also wore numerous military uniforms and caps dripping with gold braid and frogging.

PP And she adored them.

HJS Why was that? Those uniforms were so rigid and structured.

PP Uniforms suited her beautifully. Her father was in the military, and she thought of her wardrobe in terms of uniforms rather than costumes. She was the great inventor of on-screen military costumes. Whatever she wore, she was always in control. She never looked as though she'd had a fight with her outfits—unlike some other actresses—and she always wore them well.

EUGENE ROBERT RICHEE, 1933

Dietrich sang her famous song "Johnny" while wearing this costume in Mamoulian's *Song of Songs*.

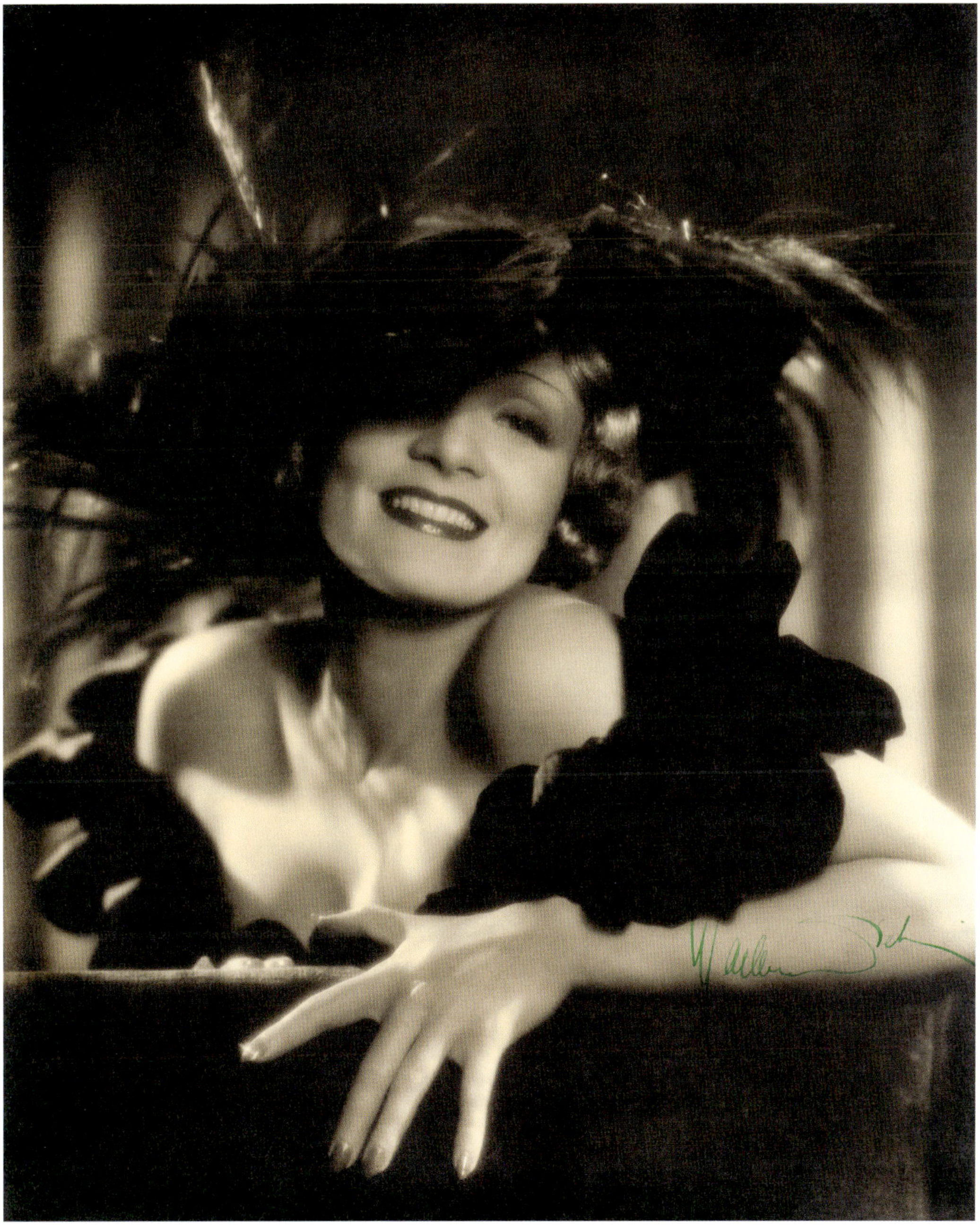

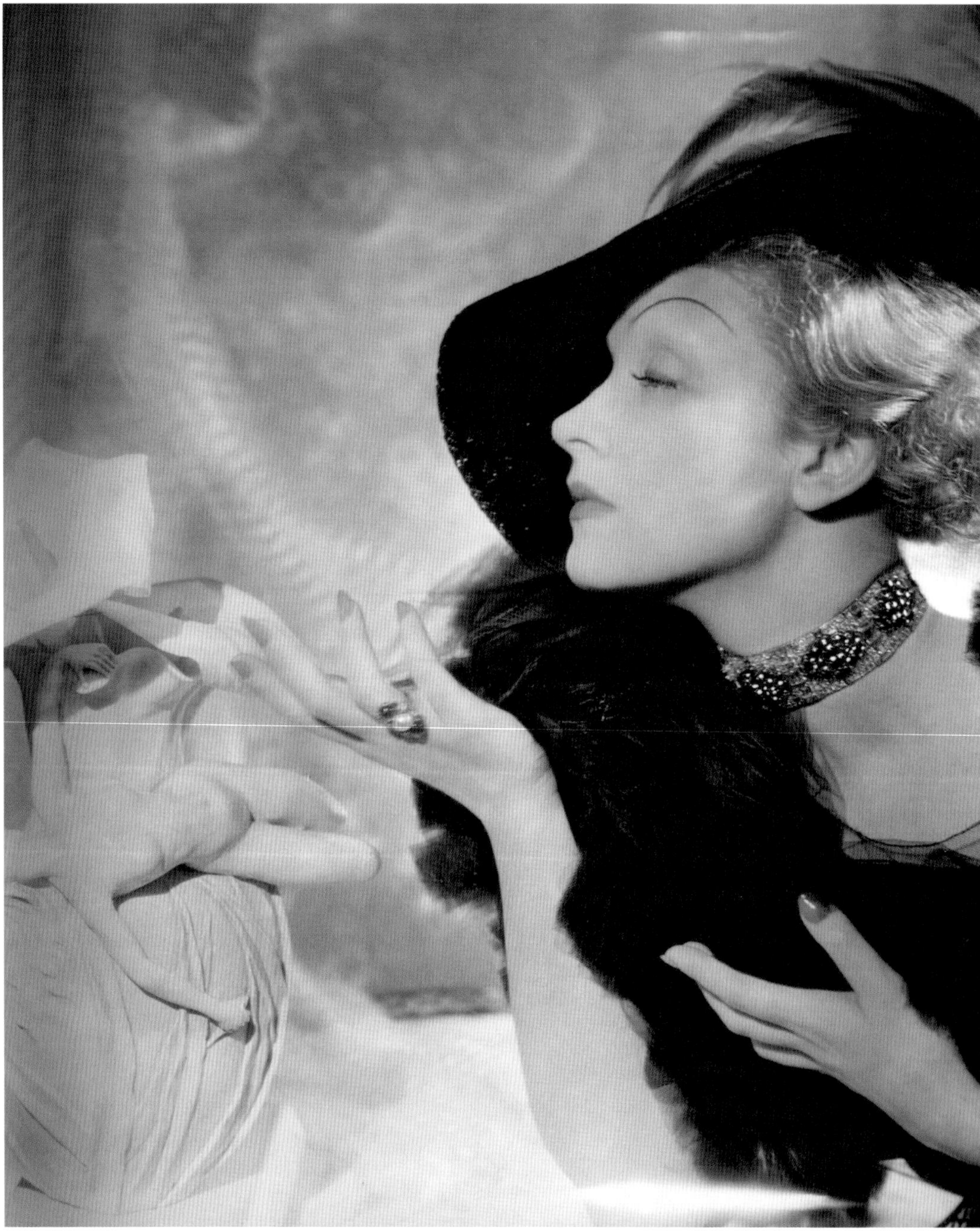

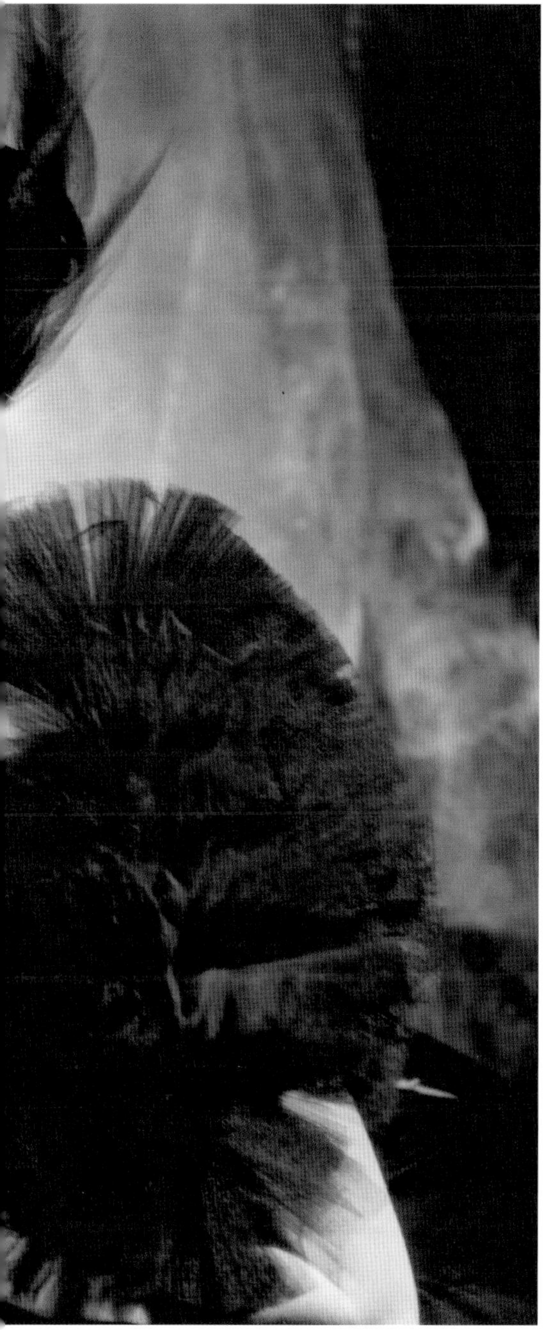

CECIL BEATON, 1935

The British society photographer Beaton was a master of stylized set design, crafting each session from scratch. He found a willing subject in Dietrich, who enjoyed his elaborate, dreamlike settings.

HJS What were her chief inspirations?

PP I can't speak about her life, as I didn't know her. And I neither can nor want to speak about her private life. But I know that she took a lot of ideas and borrowed many distinctive details from the Berlin nightclubs—havens of nonconformity in its wildest forms—that were her haunts before she fled to America. She was "discovered" and mentored by Josef von Sternberg, the genius film director who taught her the art of lighting and costume. In his memoirs, he expressed astonishment that no one had spotted the beauty that lay dormant within her, or had wanted to become her Pygmalion. She understood all these things, like the consummate professional that she was. Which led her to be very demanding. Even difficult sometimes.

HJS Was she really difficult?

PP For photographers she was a difficult model, as she set very high standards for her own performance. She did the planning and styling for many of her photographic sessions and orchestrated the way they were shot. She had it all worked out, oversaw every detail, organized everything. She wouldn't allow herself be taken in by anyone, she refused to do any poses that didn't appeal to her, and she generally laid down the law. Often she was the one who took the photographs.

HJS In other words, not a false eyelash or a strand of hair was arranged without her approval.

PP Unlike Greta Garbo, who could not have cared less about the way she was filmed, Dietrich was a technician. She would arrive on set very early, observing and checking everything. She was obsessed with her image. She needed to be perfect. She was an amazing pro, who never stopped working. She oversaw the lighting. She loved nothing more than posing head-on, looking straight at the camera lens. She would never admit to being satisfied. And she always wanted to do retakes.

EUGENE ROBERT RICHEE (Supervised by Josef von Sternberg), 1932

Dietrich's publicity portraits for *Desire* are among the best of her career. Her glamour is innate and effortless.

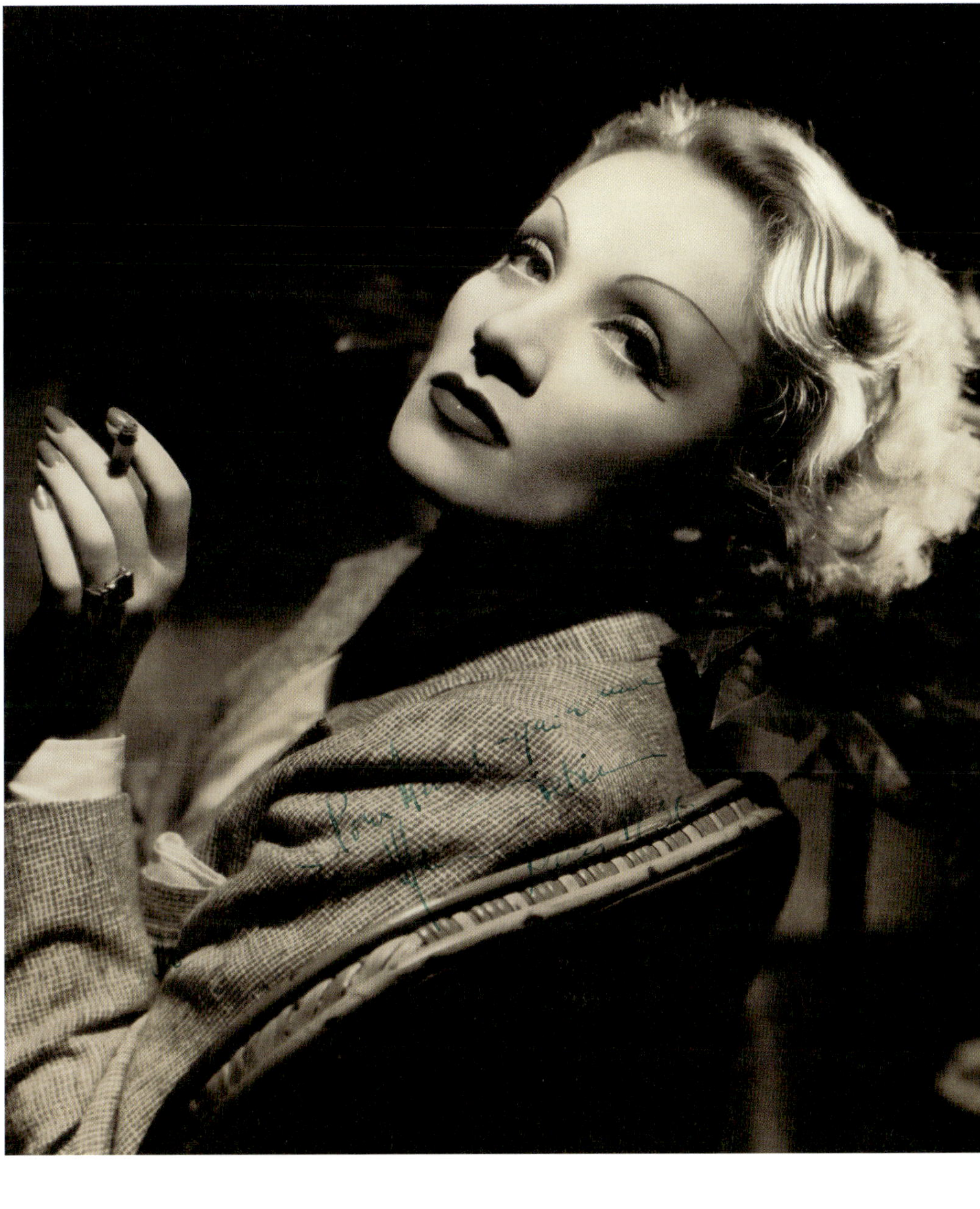

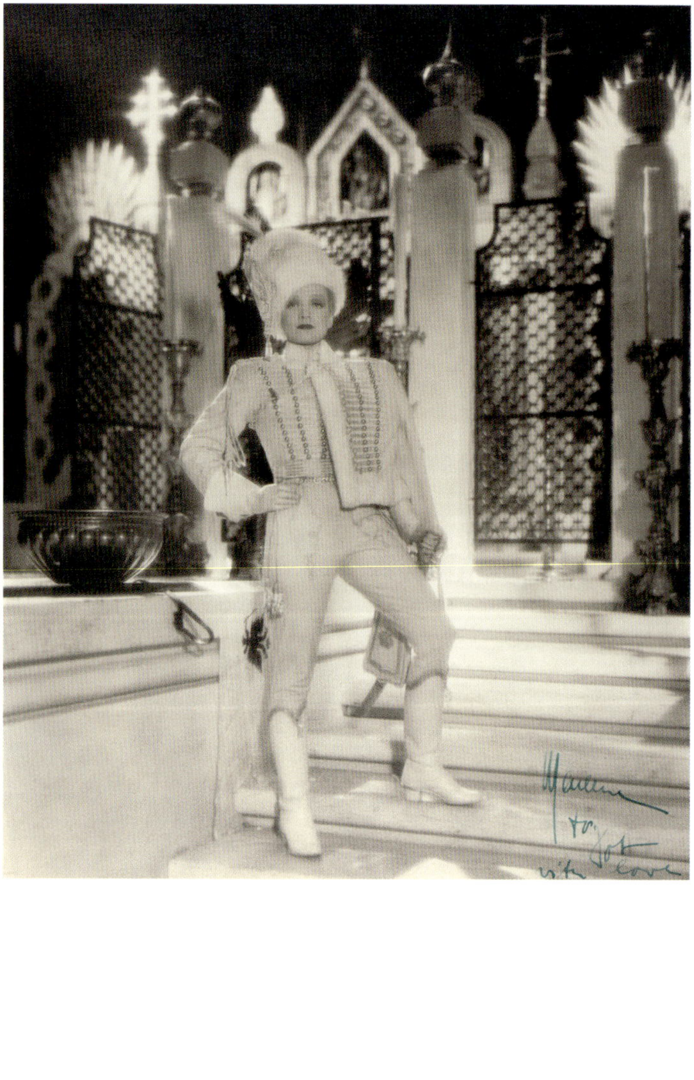

WILLIAM WALLING, JR., 1934

In late 1933, Dietrich posed in a Travis Banton costume on the set of *Catherine the Great*. In May 1934, the film was retitled *The Scarlet Empress* to avoid confusion with the Alexander Korda production *The Rise of Catherine the Great*.

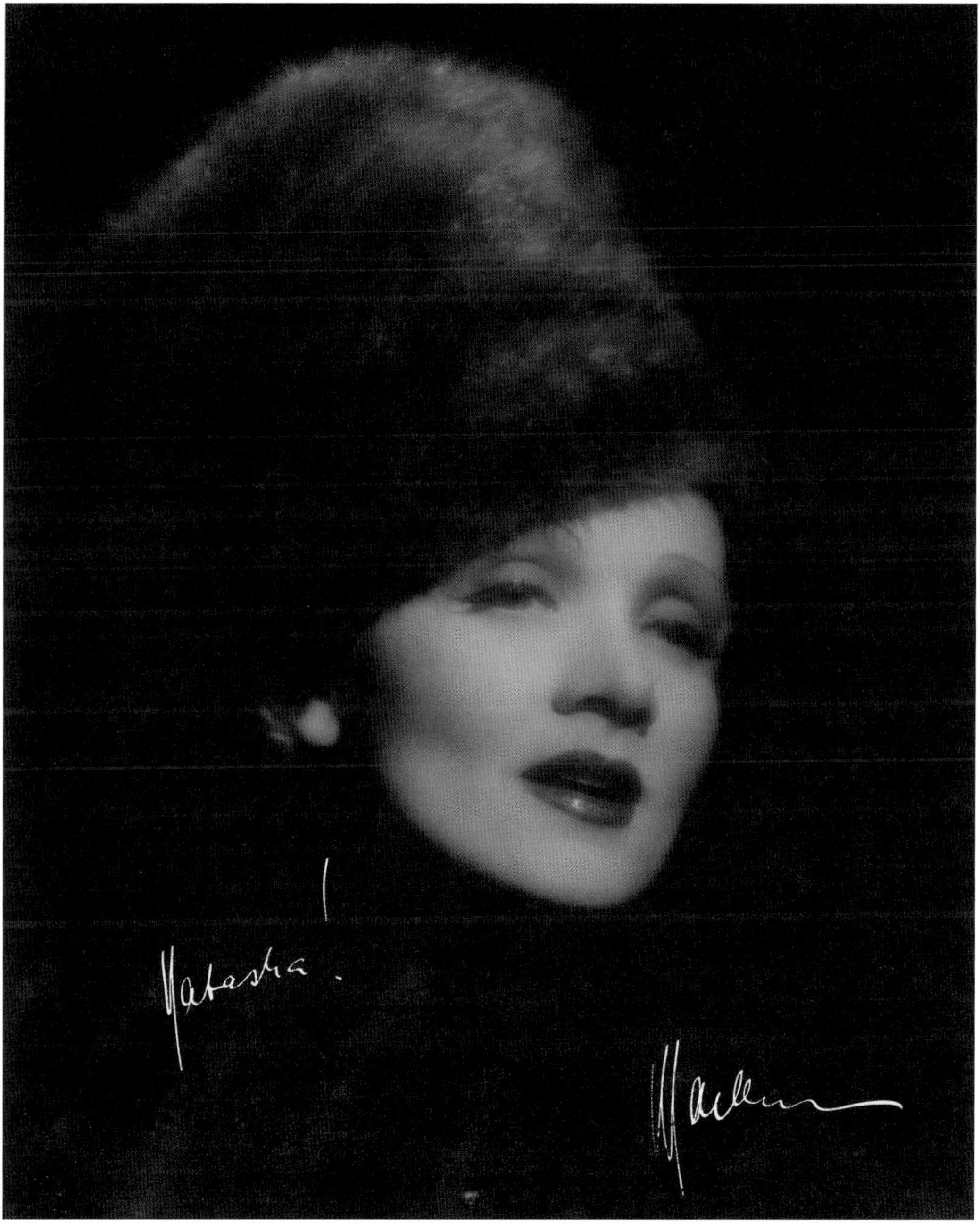

WILLIAM WALLING, JR. (Supervised by Josef von Sternberg), 1934

The Scarlet Empress was Sternberg's sexy interpretation of Russia's Catherine the Great. It was the sixth of his films with Dietrich, and their last before studio censorship restricted the subject matter of their films.

UNSIGNED PHOTOGRAPH, 1938

After parting from Paramount in 1937, Dietrich spent more than a year in Europe. While there, she continued to accommodate photographers.

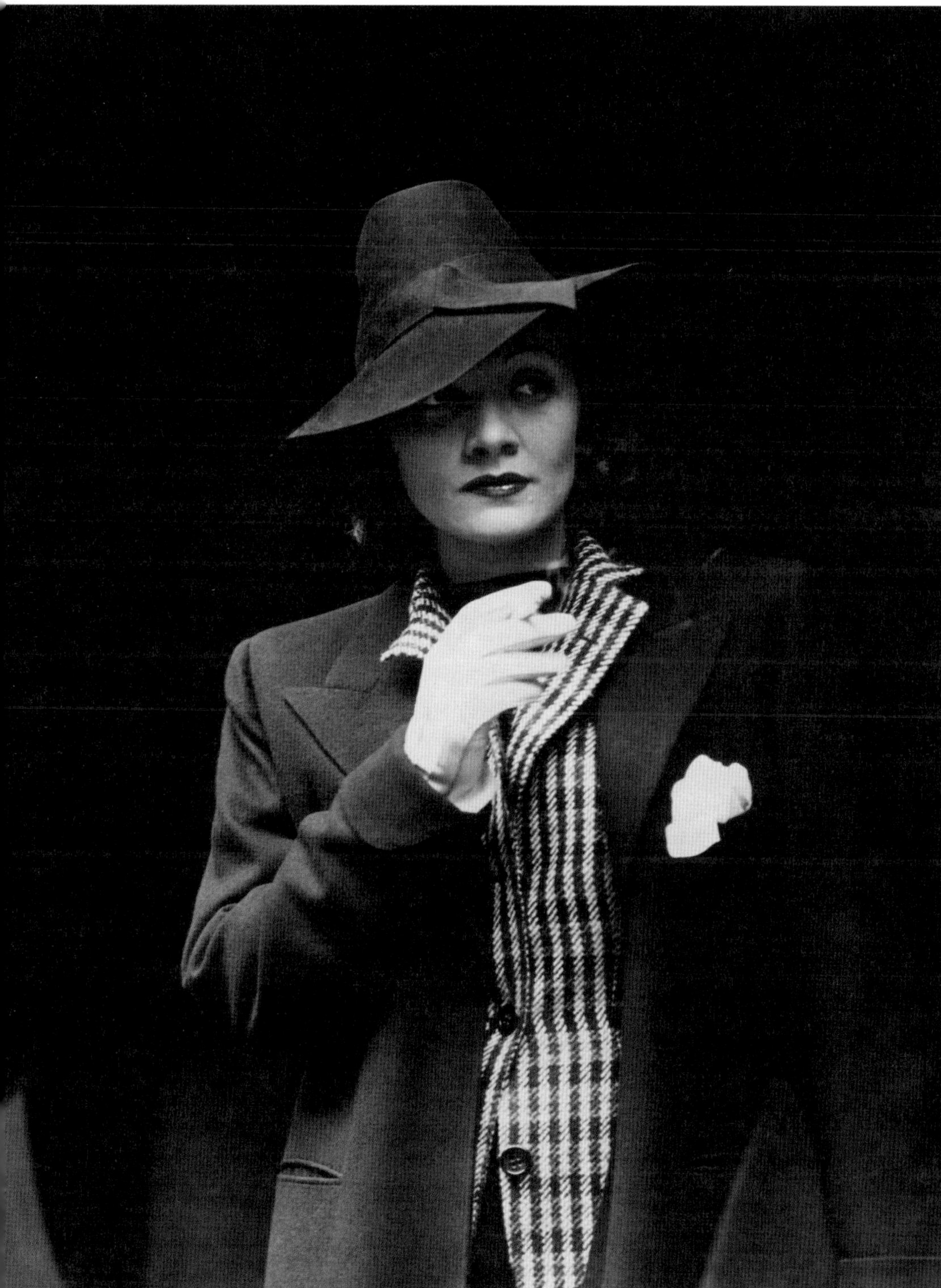

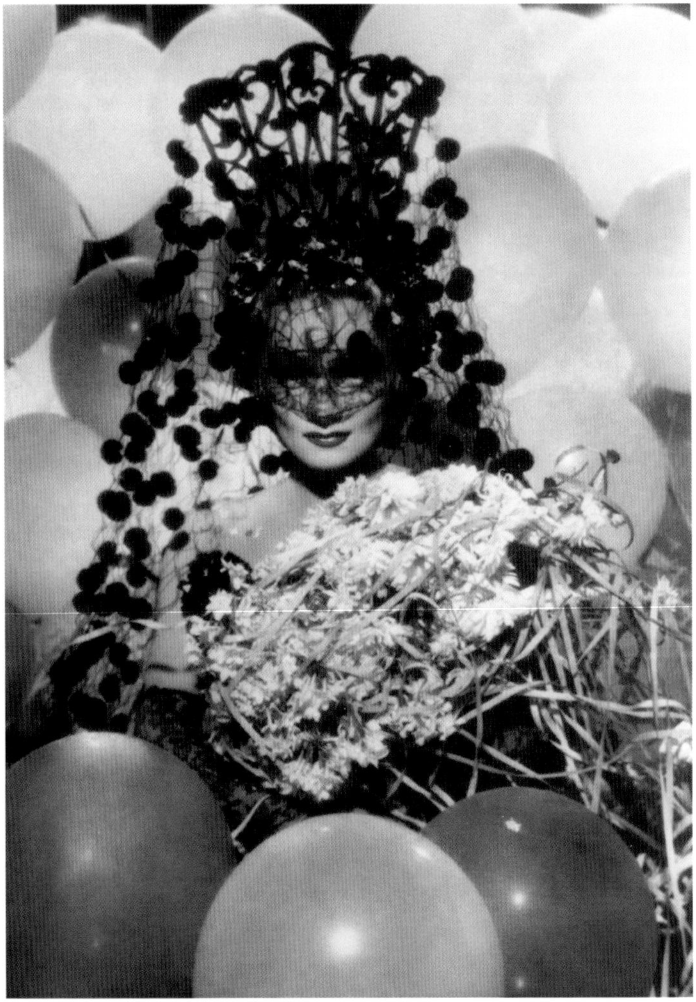

DON ENGLISH (Supervised by Josef von Sternberg), 1935

The Devil Is a Woman was Sternberg's adaptation of the Pierre Louÿs novel *La Femme et le Pantin*. The last of Sternberg's seven films with Dietrich, it remains a masterwork of design, costume, and photography.

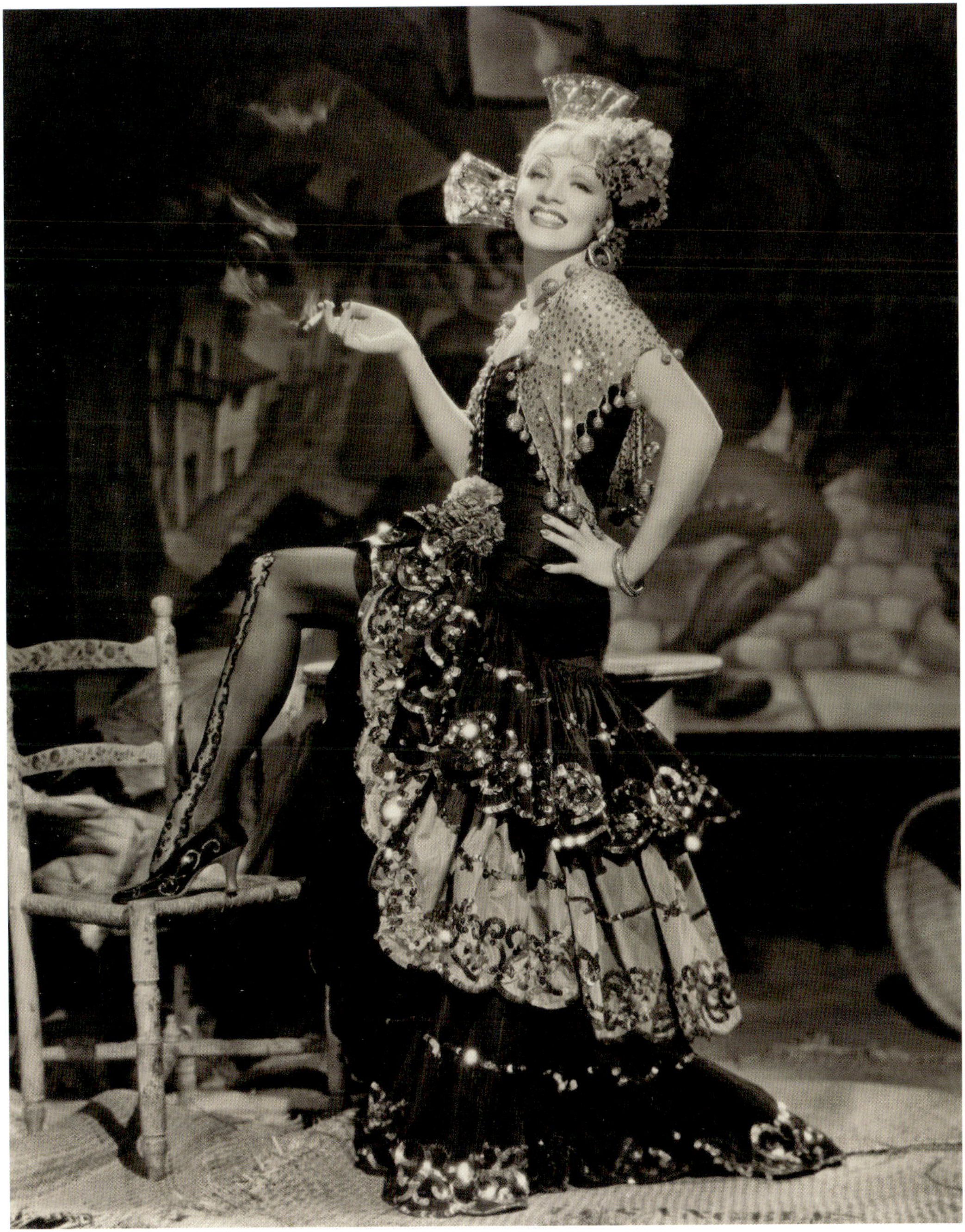

DON ENGLISH (Supervised by Josef von Sternberg), 1935

When asked the title of her favorite film, Dietrich for years named *The Devil Is a Woman*. She felt that she looked more beautiful in it than in any other. She was really invested in this production and created the costumes featured above and on page 40.

HJS Her love of display, her delight in performance—she owed these to Josef von Sternberg, who established her on set and mentored her style. She worked relentlessly, as everyone agrees, but she always took the time and trouble to express the gratitude she felt to Sternberg.

PP Whenever Sternberg was mentioned in her presence, and whenever she spoke of him, Dietrich was always intelligent enough to acknowledge what she owed him, how much she owed him.

HJS Starting with her physical appearance ...

PP It was Sternberg who made her lose weight, who slimmed her down, and changed her body shape. Between the filming of *The Blue Angel* in Germany and *Morocco*, her first Hollywood film in 1930, she shed weight, the result of the diet that he had put her on and that she had followed to the letter. He took a relatively plump actress and conjured up, from her first Hollywood film, a star who was willowy and slender. After they arrived in America, Sternberg demanded that *The Blue Angel*—already on release in Europe—should be shown in the United States only after the release of *Morocco*, which was her second film. So American audiences saw a slimmer actress who conformed better to Californian notions of what was desirable.

KENNETH ALEXANDER, 1936

Dietrich went to Yuma, Arizona, to film exterior scenes with director Richard Boleslawski for *The Garden of Allah*, which was Hollywood's second three-strip Technicolor feature.

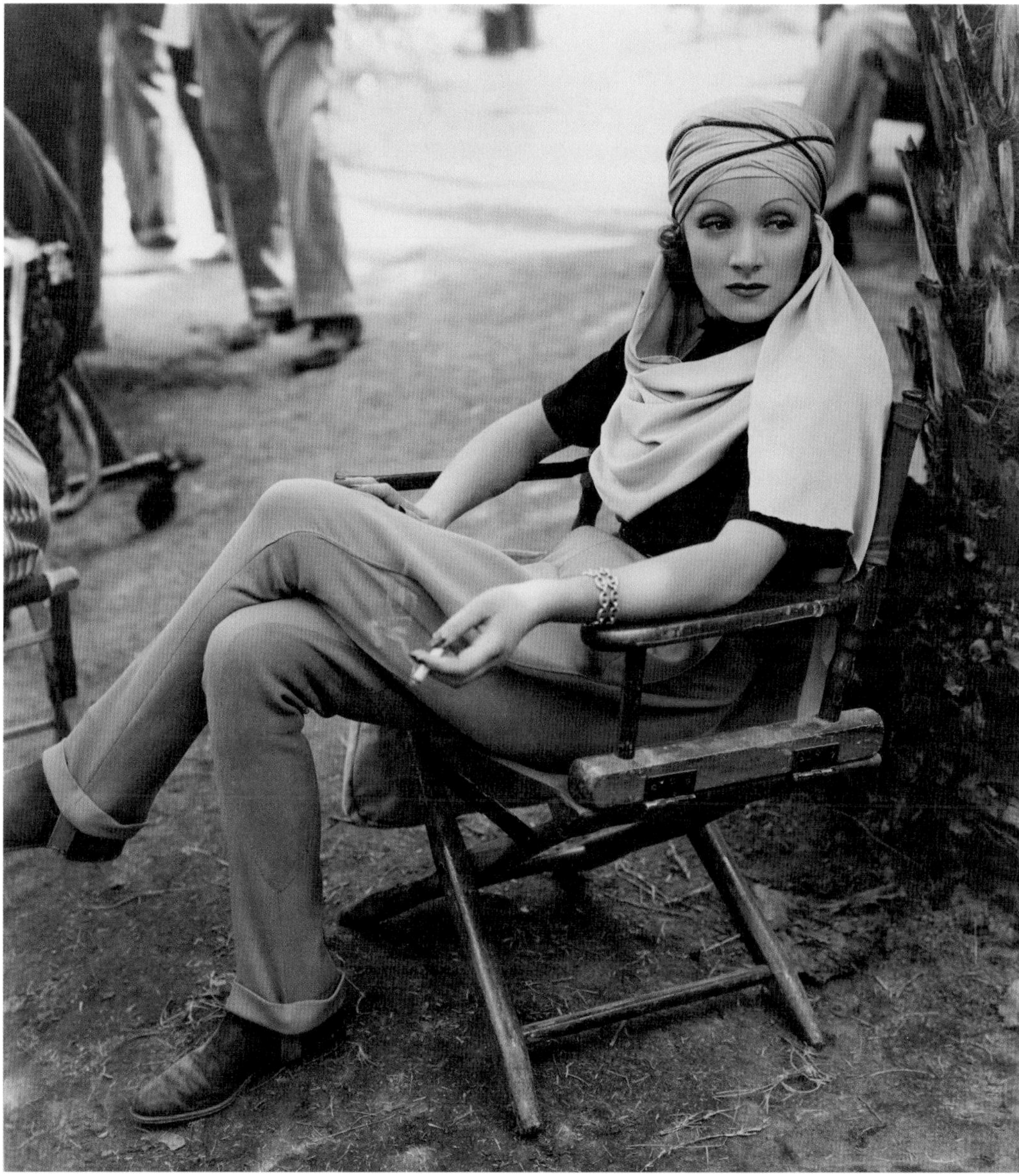

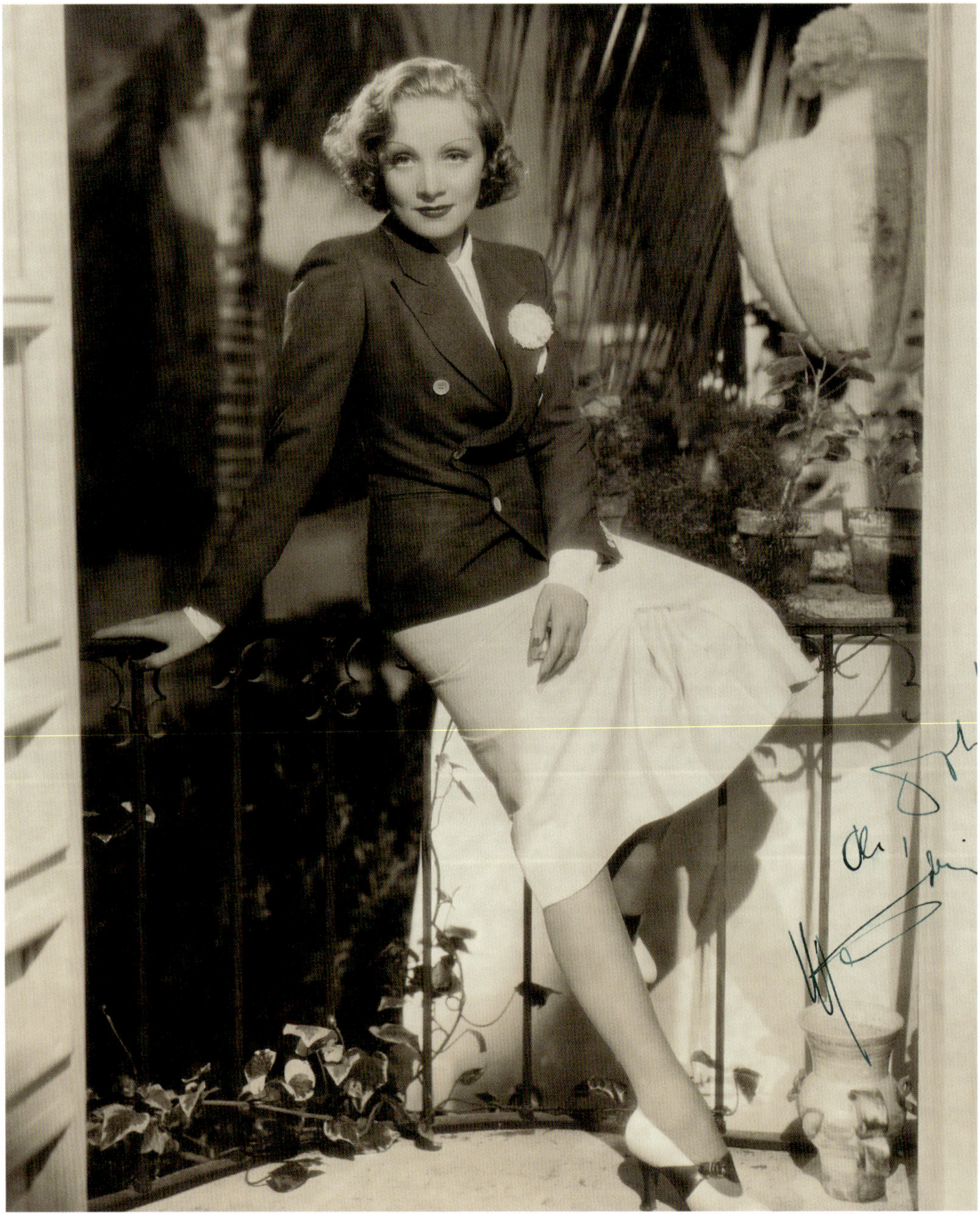

DON ENGLISH, 1936

In Frank Borzage's *Desire*, Dietrich wore this Travis Banton suit. He was responsible for the lovely gowns she wore in her Paramount films.

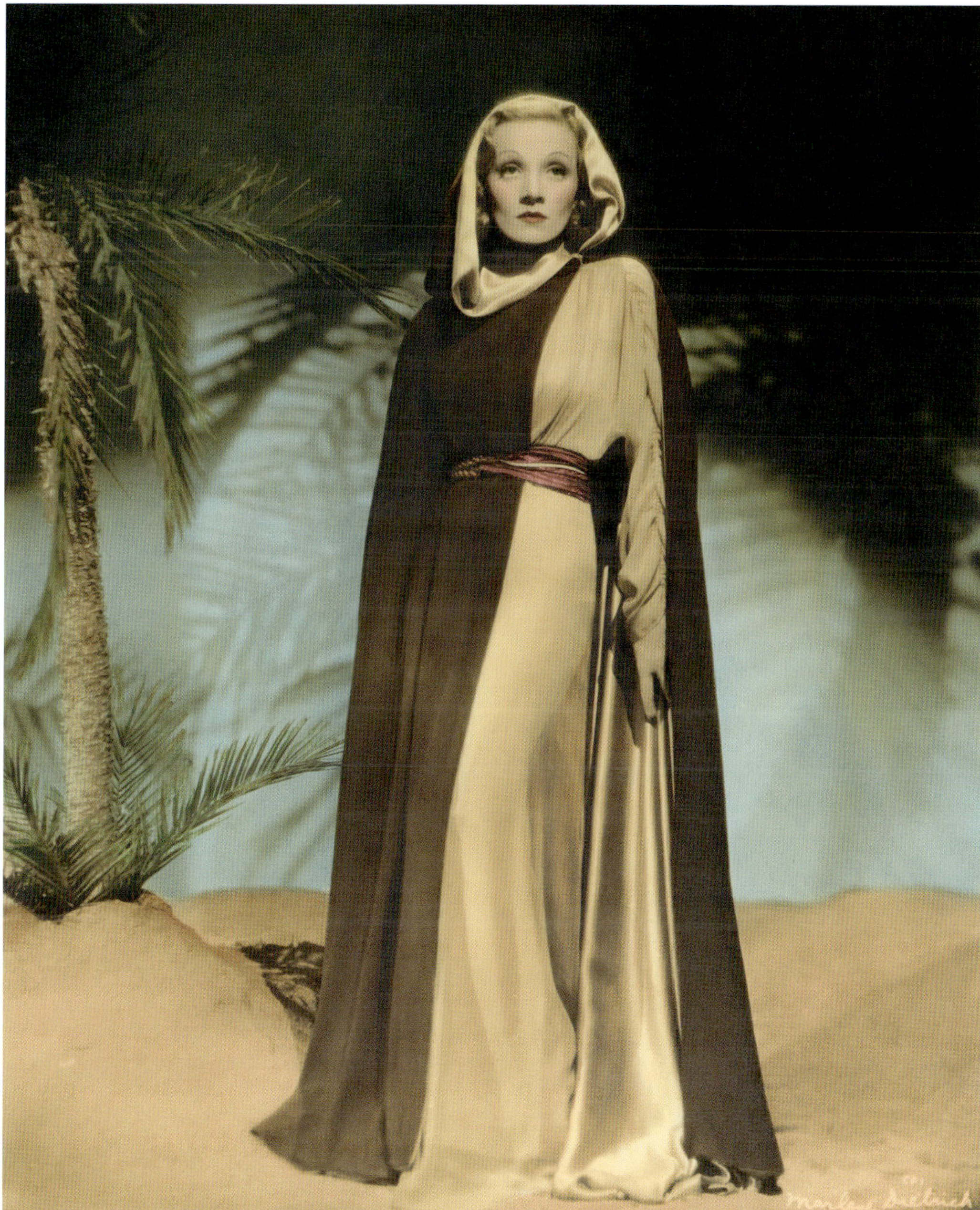

KENNETH ALEXANDER, 1936

This portrait was made for David O. Selznick's Technicolor production of Richard Boleslawski's *The Garden of Allah*. The portrait was shot with black-and-white film but stencil-colored later.

HJS Was Dietrich herself concerned about looking more desirable?

PP No. She displayed a deep contempt for sexuality as an end in itself. She liked to think of herself as a woman who was intelligent, loving, and mistress of her own choices, demonstrating once again that was ahead of her time.

HJS Did she owe this to her education as a fighter, to her upbringing in a military family?

PP She was disciplined and ethical in her approach, and she did, indeed, owe this to her education and to her military family. Her father, Louis Otto Dietrich, was a Prussian officer and lieutenant in the Imperial police, who gave his two daughters (Marlene had an older sister, Elisabeth) a very strict upbringing. Discipline was de rigueur in the family home. Louis Otto Dietrich, who was bisexual, died in 1908. His widow Wilhelmina married his best friend, another Prussian officer, a captain in the cavalry. He died in 1917, before he was able to adopt the two girls, as he had intended. Marlene had a tough upbringing in an unconventional family. She owed her emotional development to her French nanny, who taught her love and kindness, qualities that had been stifled beneath this military carapace.

HJS So Dietrich was a little soldier, in a way?

PP Dietrich was a real little soldier, a warrior, even in her most romantic moments. She was a soldier who liked impeccable outfits, who obeyed orders, and who in turn gave a lot of orders, adding copious amounts of tips and advice. Arriving on set at the earliest possible moment, she would lose no time in charming the cameramen, working with them until they achieved a result that was to the complete satisfaction of both sides. On set, whether shooting a film or photographs, she behaved as though she was waging war, concentrating all her energies on a single goal—that of being herself, and not just another actress.

DON ENGLISH, 1936

Frank Borzage's *Desire* was the funny, glamorous vehicle Dietrich needed after Sternberg ended their collaboration. Ernst Lubitsch produced the film, and his famous touch is visible throughout.

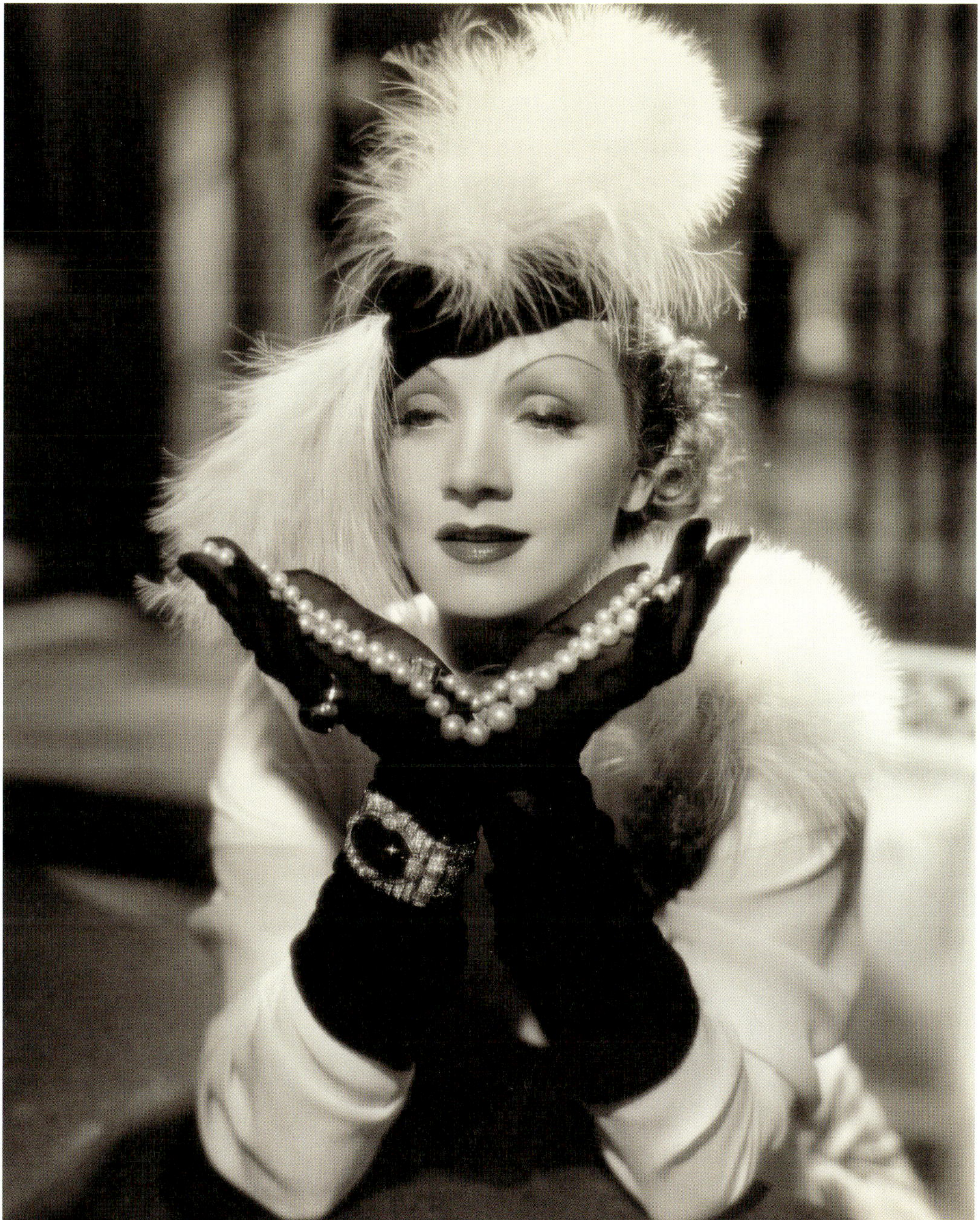

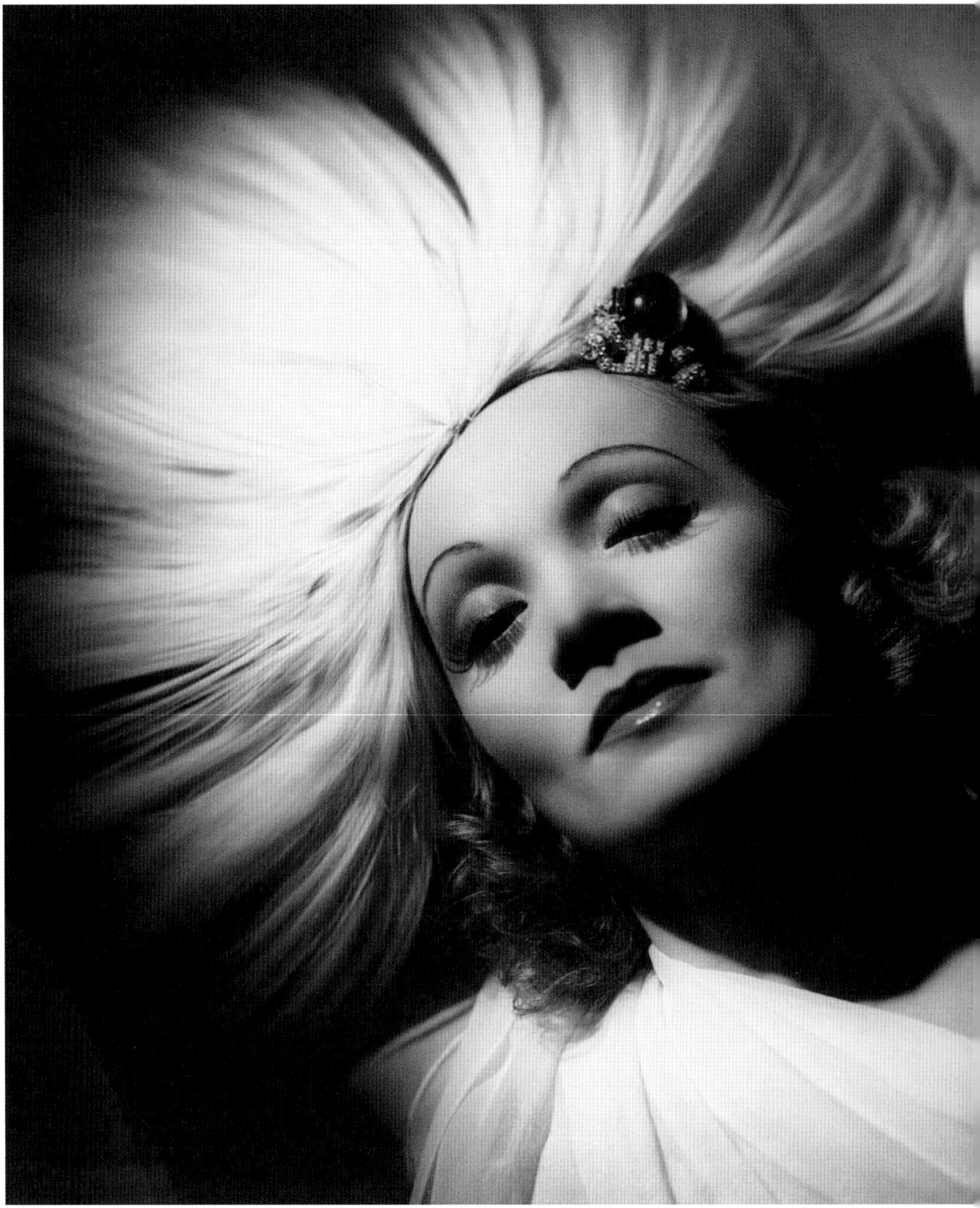

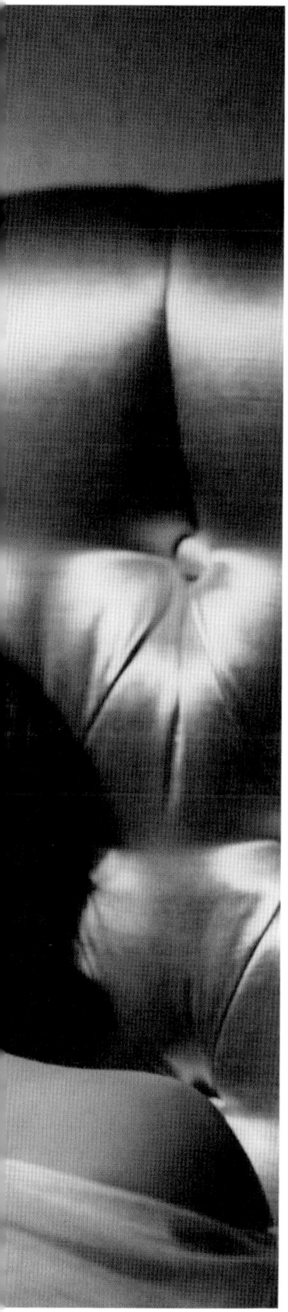

GEORGE HURRELL, 1937

Hurrell's work with Dietrich found new exposure in 1980 when it became the first of his limited-edition images to sell from the G. Ray Hawkins Gallery in Hollywood. It helped launch his second career.

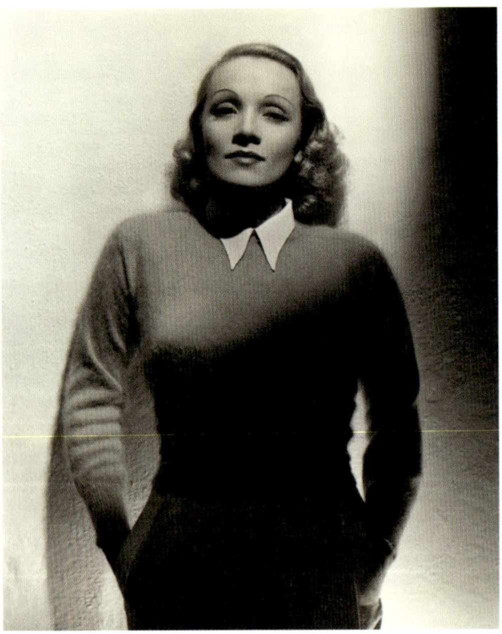

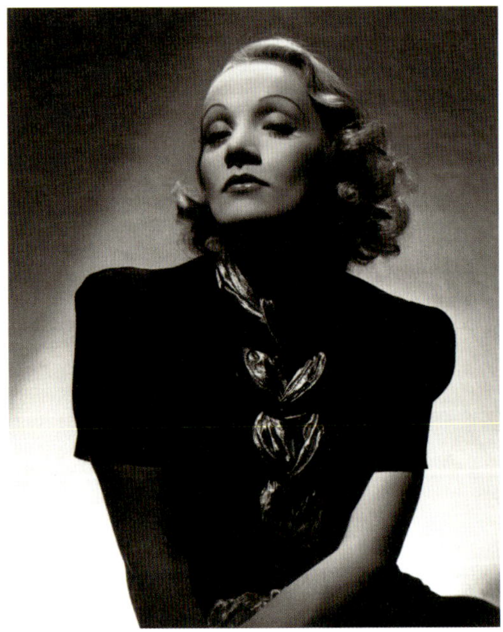

GEORGE HURRELL, 1937

Hurrell found Dietrich exacting and demanding, but he acceded to her requirements, which included a full-length mirror angled so she could see her exact pose. Once she had it, she would say, "Shoot, George! Shoot!"

GEORGE HURRELL, 1937

This portrait was made in Hurrell's Sunset Boulevard studio. On the eve of her departure from Paramount Pictures, Dietrich commissioned this session in order to create a new image of herself.

SCOTTY WELBOURNE, 1941

Warner Bros. publicity required a certain number of sporty, bright images from each session, so Dietrich acquiesced.

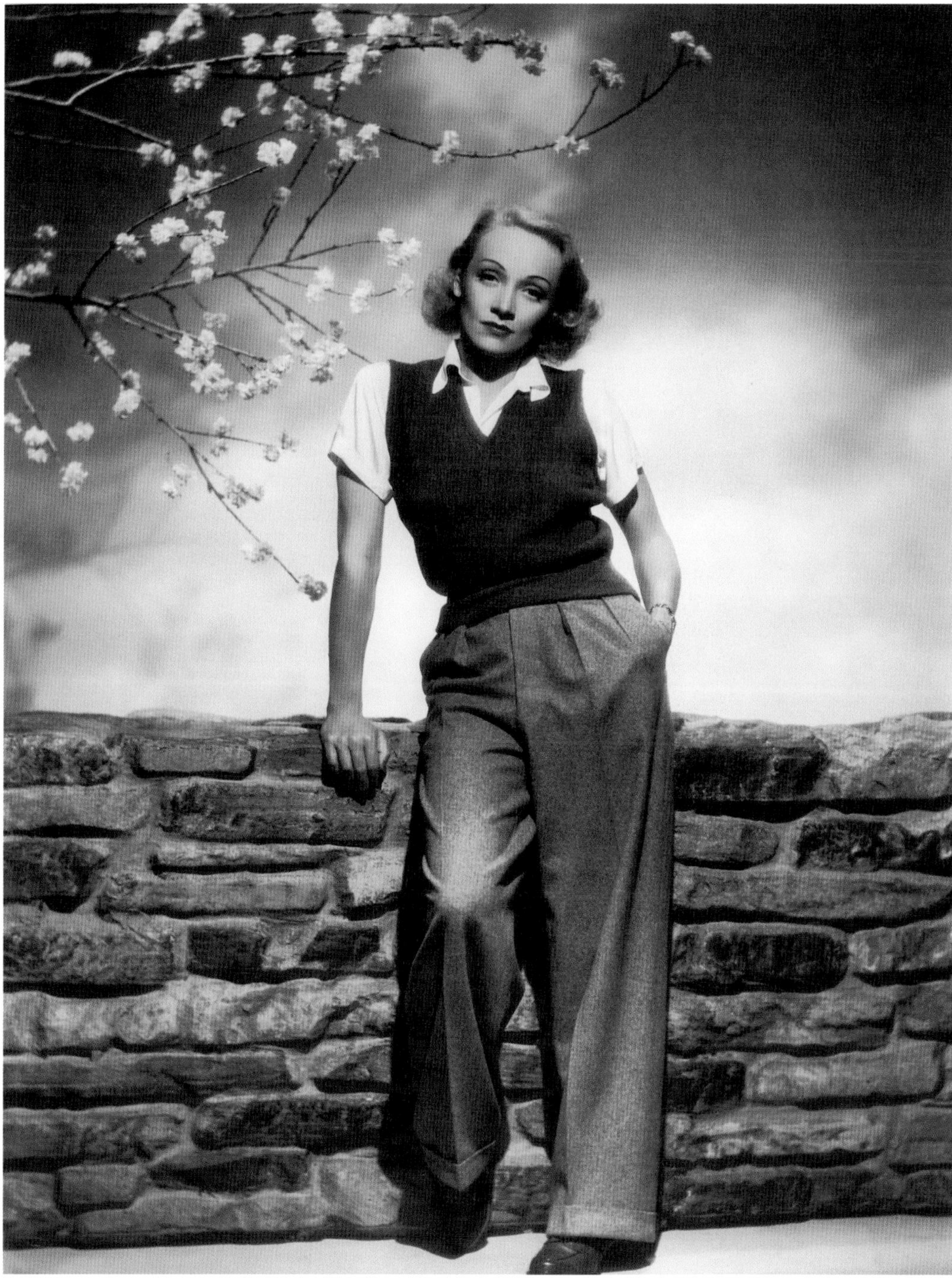

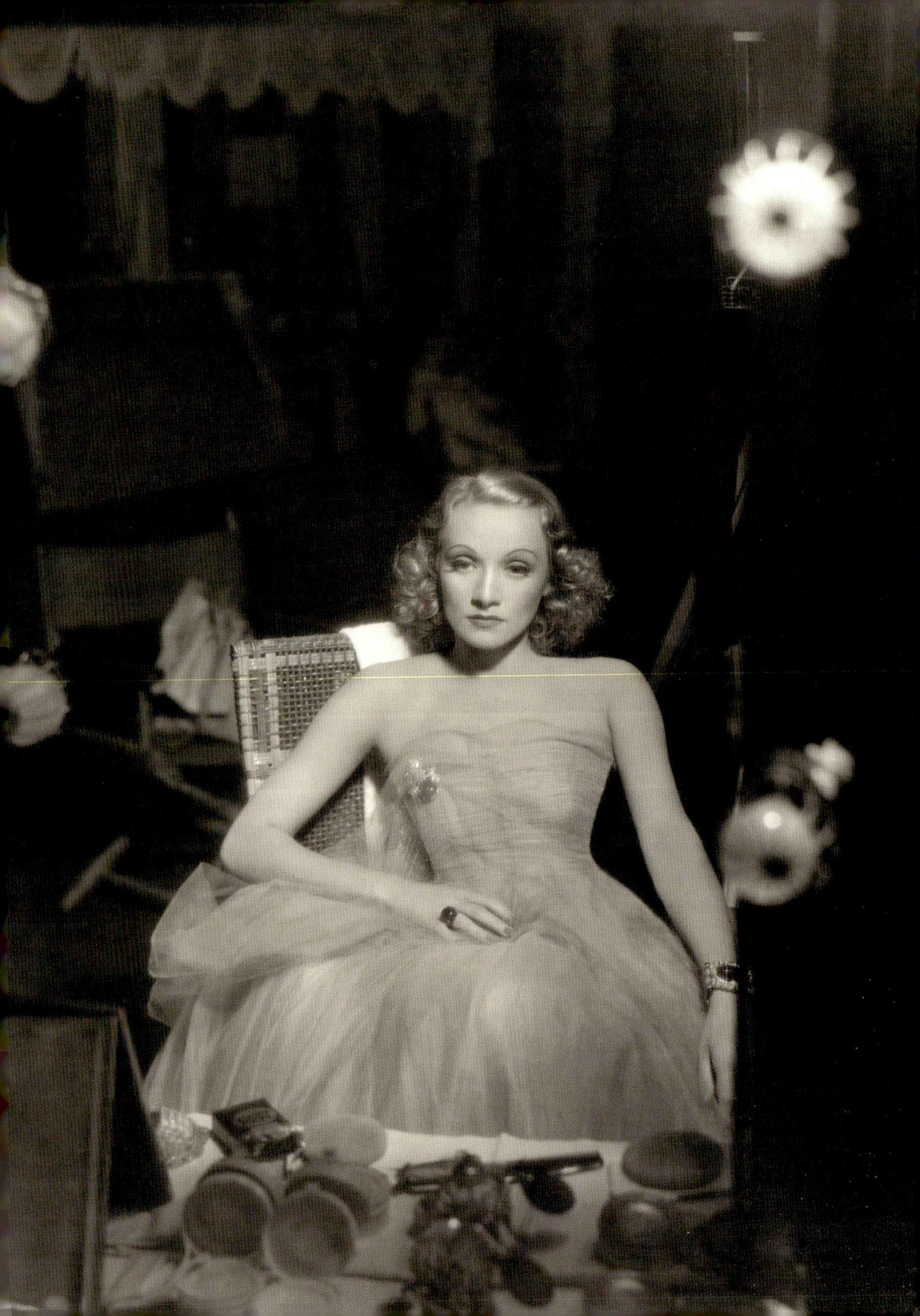

HJS In all situations, whatever the circumstances, she conducted herself like a conqueror sweeping all before her. When you were in her orbit you had to stay in step and toe the line.

PP Audiences could sense that both in her life and internally that she had a sort of inner architecture or skeleton, a backbone that would keep everything securely upright and aloft, through sheer effort of will and certainly not any divine intervention. It was this unbending backbone that dictated who she was, that shaped her, and imposed an iron discipline. Unlike Marilyn Monroe, for example, there was nothing unbalanced about her.

HJS Did she retain this iron discipline throughout her life, and did it help her to combat the effects of aging?

PP Her final years were occupied, preoccupied one might say, with her struggle against encroaching age. She hated it when people called her "the world's sexiest grandmother." It used to drive her crazy. She wanted only one thing, which was to be seductive for as long as possible. To the point that when she felt she no longer had either the disposition or the looks for it, she withdrew into complete seclusion. When she didn't want to see anyone any more, she dropped the curtain on her performance and drew the curtains on her life. For the last fifteen years of her life she shut herself away in her apartment on avenue Montaigne in Paris, at first in her large bedroom overlooking the street and later in a room overlooking the rear.

HJS Few people are aware that she spent the final years of her life confined to bed. She could no longer walk. What did she do to occupy herself? Did she dream about her fame, which was still very much alive?

PP She thought that old age was cruel, that it was dragging her to her grave, and that she absolutely was not ready to give up on life. She would return in her mind to her Berlin years, when she exuded the spirit of the times—*l'air du temps*—and when she was the very height of fashion. In memory of that era, she would read the newspapers and make countless phone calls, lifting the receiver from her bed, punching in the numbers, making believe, as she lay in the confines of her bed, that she was drifting from one room to the next on calls to everyone under the sun.

DON ENGLISH (Supervised by Josef von Sternberg), 1937

Making the romantic film *Angel* with the brilliant director Lubitsch should have been a joy for Dietrich, but the constant rewrites demanded by the censors caused the filmmakers to lose their zest.

"Her success is out of all proportion and yet it is entirely due to her perseverance that she is not just an old discarded film star. She magnetizes her audience and mesmerizes them (and herself) into believing in her."

CECIL BEATON, *THE UNEXPURGATED BEATON DIARIES*, 2003.

CECIL BEATON, 1935

Dietrich was fond of Cartier jewelry and enjoyed wearing it during sessions. She was a good friend of Jeanne Toussaint, jeweller and director of Cartier partly because of her efforts during war.

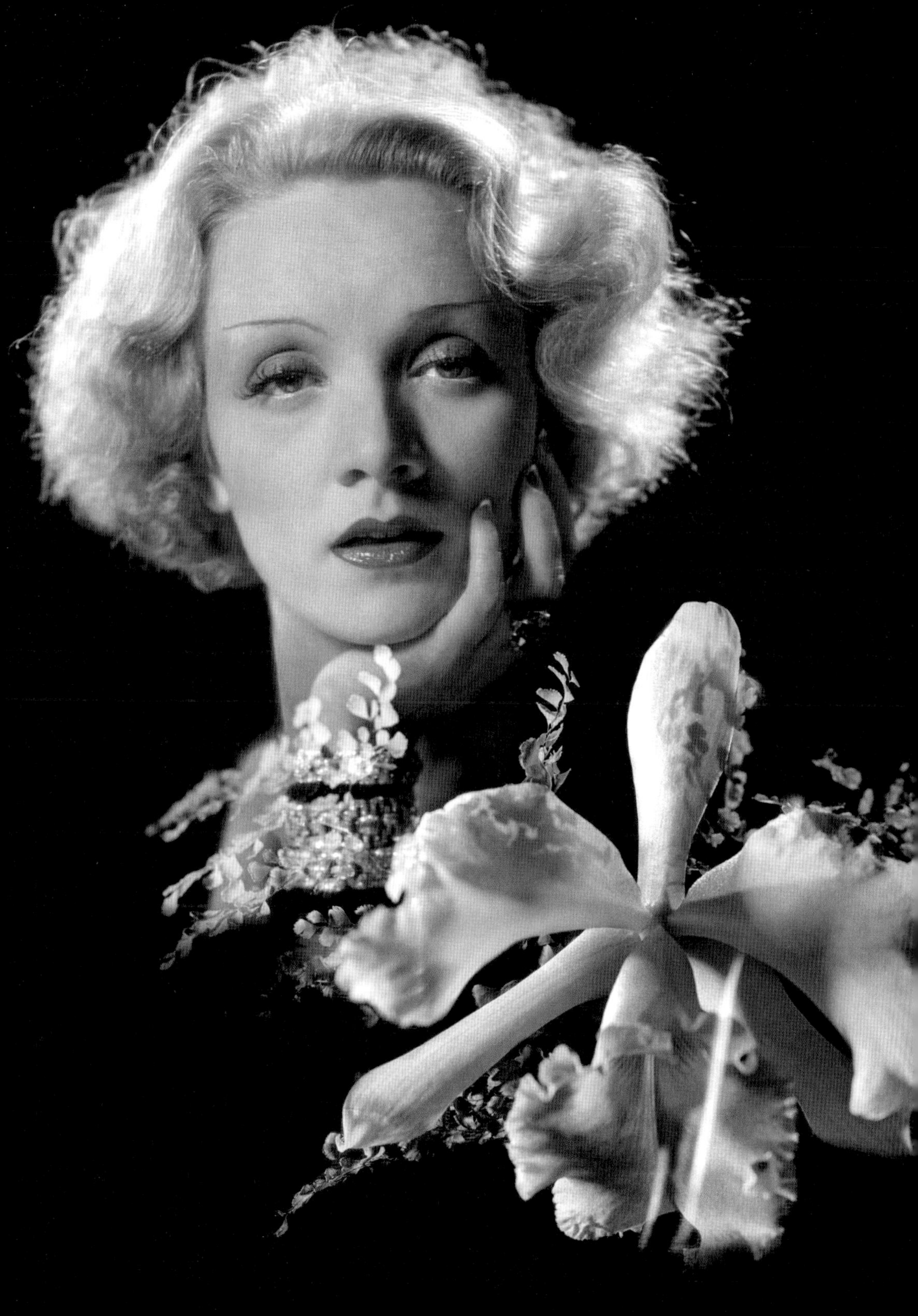

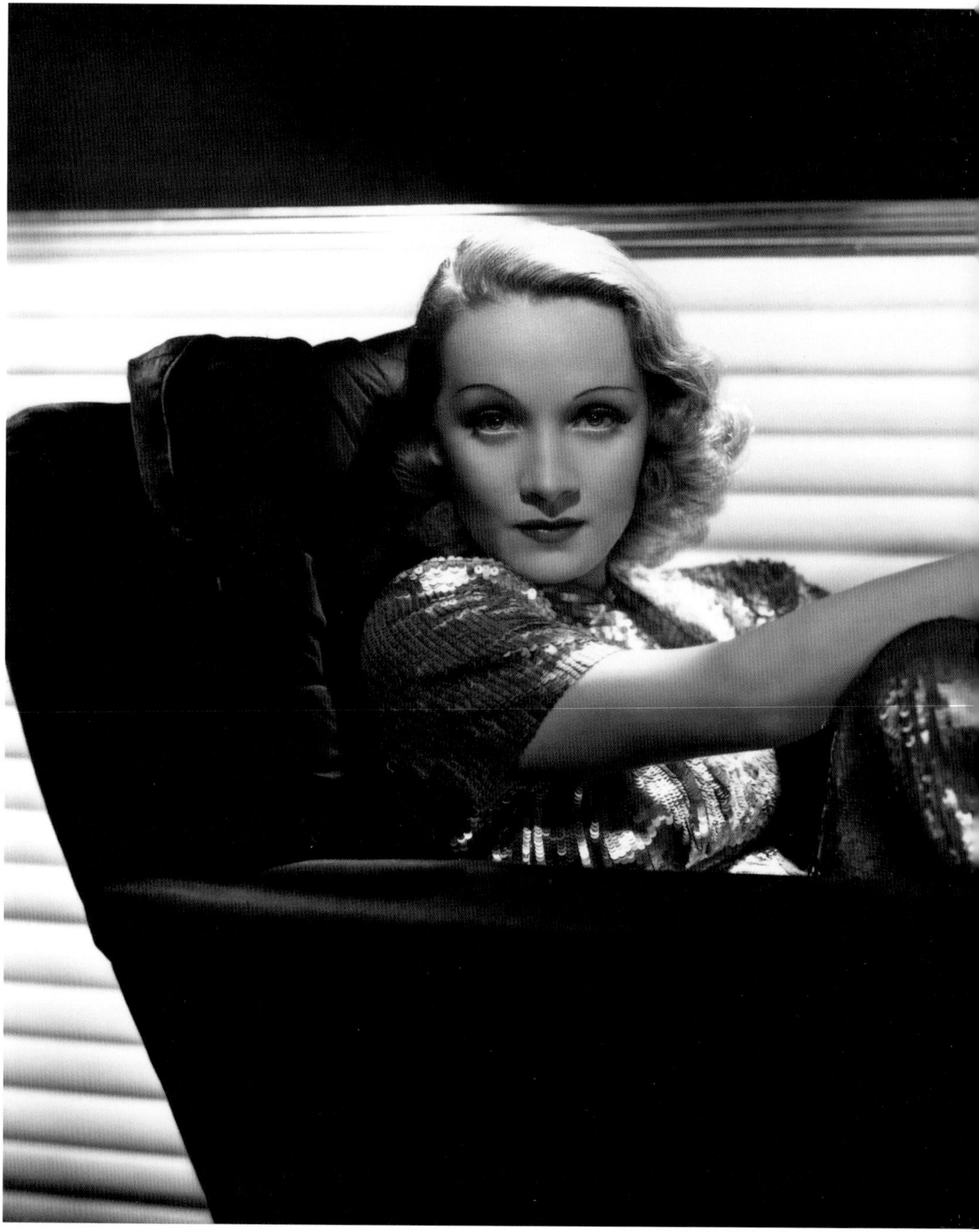

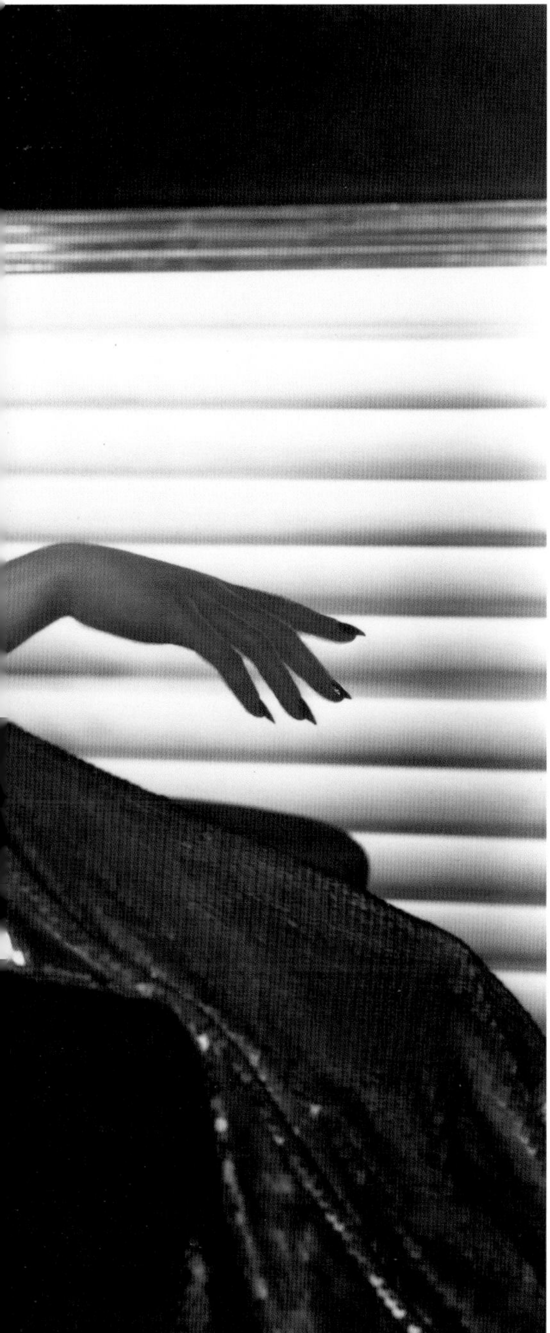

GEORGE HURRELL, 1937

"I never knew a dame who was so hot for pictures of herself," said Hurrell years later, as he recalled Dietrich's willingness to pose for an entire day, and her eagerness to see the proofs.

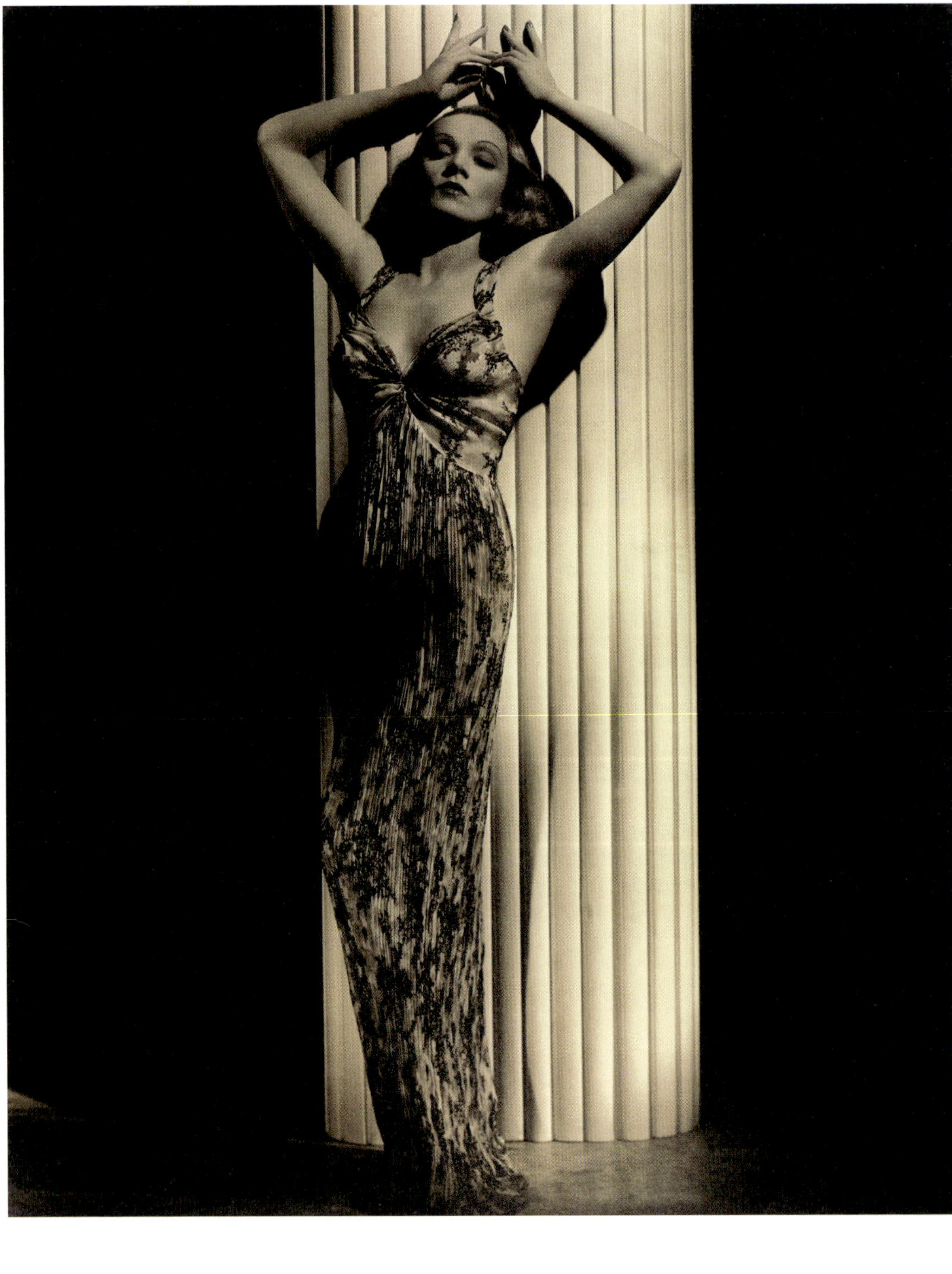

GEORGE HURRELL, 1937

This alluring series was made during Dietrich's marathon session in Hurrell's Sunset Boulevard studio.

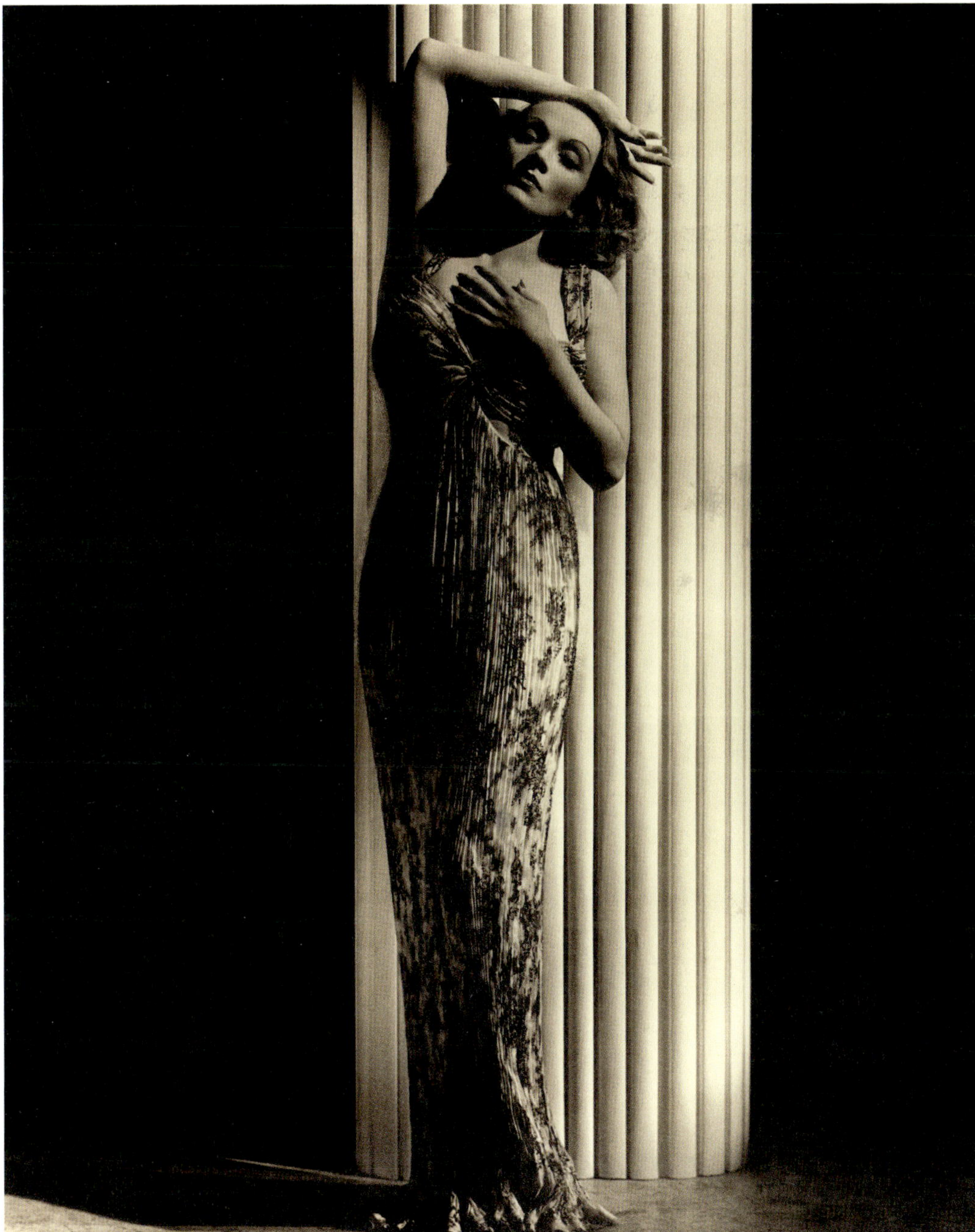

GEORGE HURRELL, 1937

This portrait was shot in Hurrell's Sunset Boulevard studio during Dietrich's long day of work there. In this shot, Dietrich is most likely perfecting her pose by looking at her reflection in a full-length mirror.

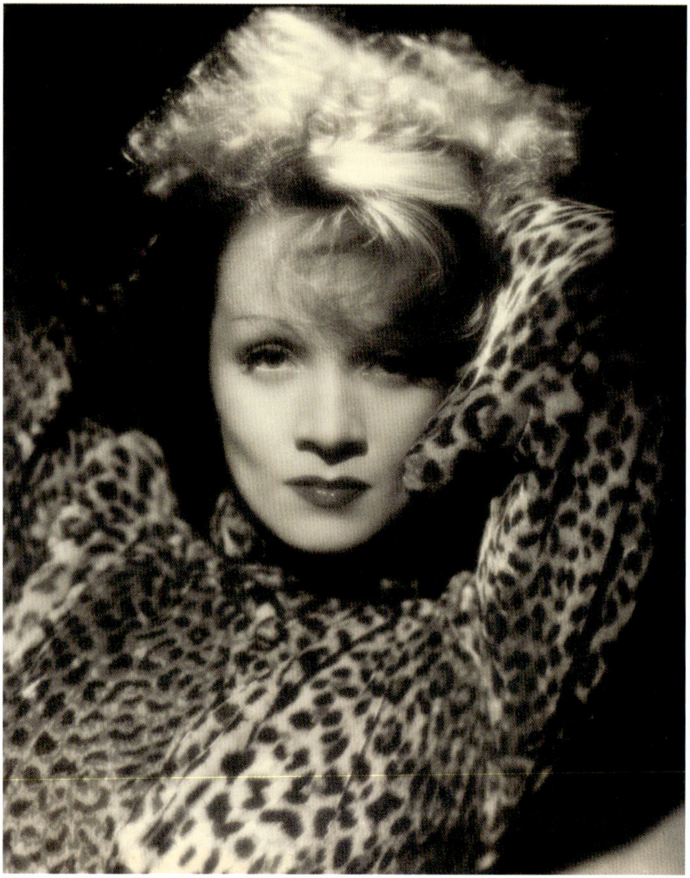

JOHN ENGSTEAD, 1939

Dietrich first wore this leopard-print dress in her session with George Hurrell, so this portrait is often misattributed to Hurrell, but he never used the diffused lighting seen in this portrait.

JOHN ENGSTEAD, 1939

This was one of John Engstead's first portraits of Dietrich. They would work together for nearly twenty years.

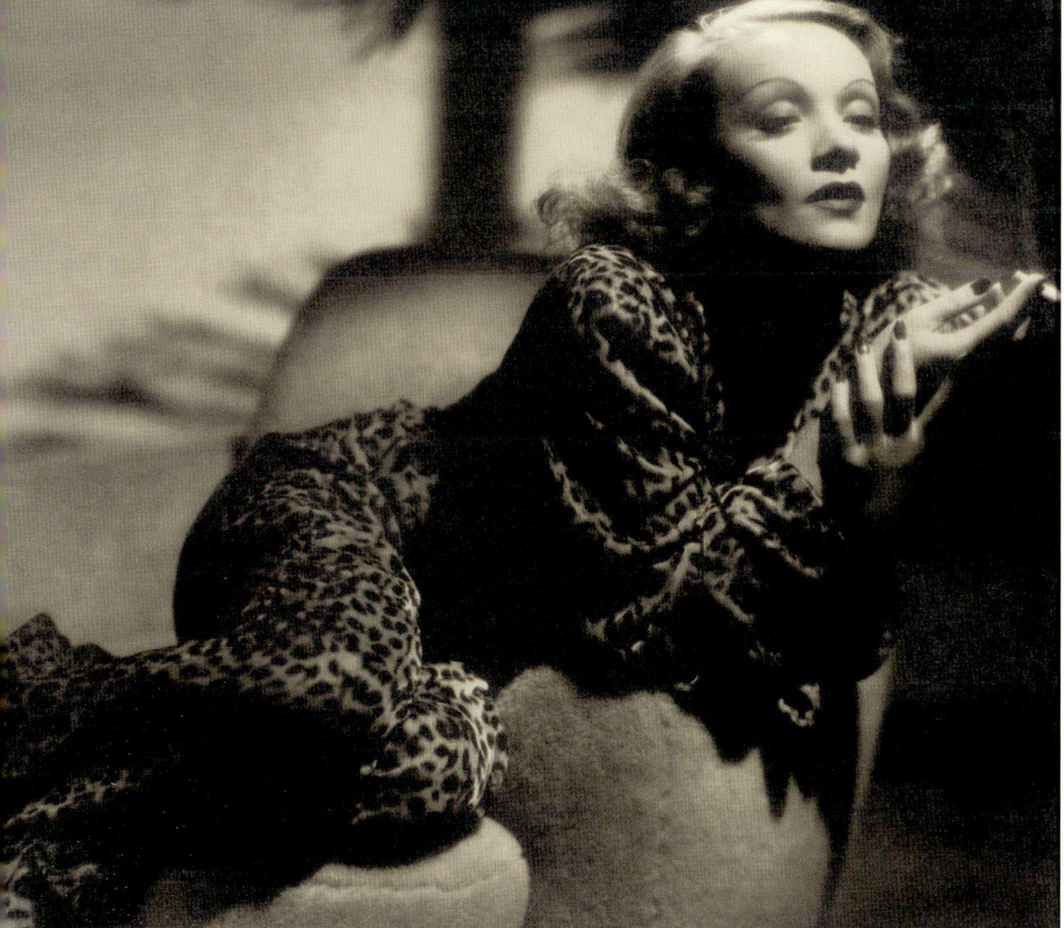

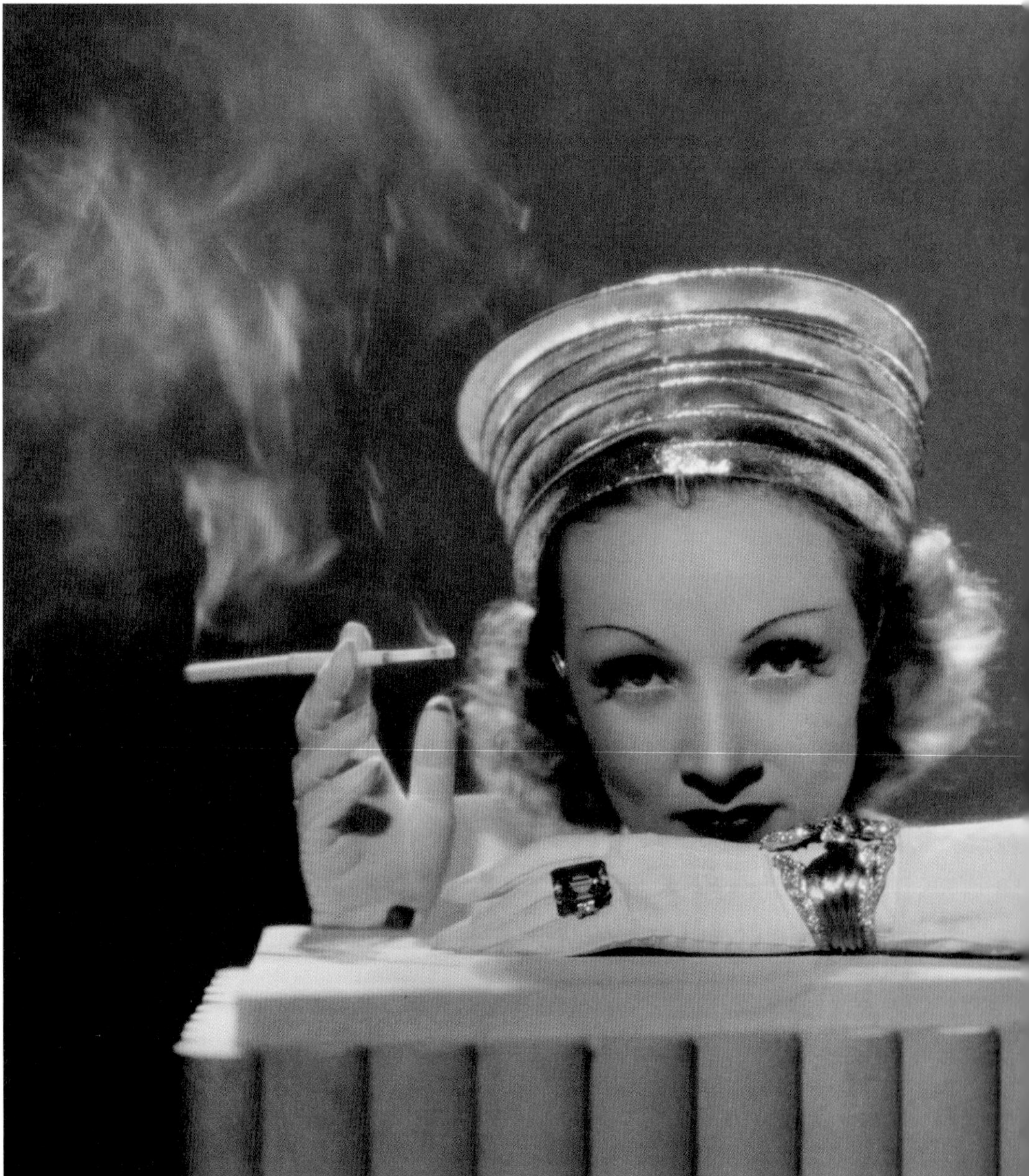

RAY JONES, 1941

The image of Dietrich that Jones created was no less glamorous than Sternberg's image ten years earlier, but Dietrich's films for Universal made her a down-to-earth character, rather than a flamboyant and exotic personality.

HJS Did she distinguish between reality and romanticism, the two poles between which her life never ceased to oscillate?

PP She had a profoundly rooted sense of reality. Dietrich was a deeply practical woman, who was also steeped in a true romanticism. Throughout her life she remained a romantic, through and through. A little sentimental and naïve, even. Matters of the flesh were of little significance to her, but matters of love and the heart were deeply important. For her, only that which made her soul tremble was truly genuine. I know this from two of my friends who were close to her, the photographers Patrice Calmettes and François-Marie Banier, who still have great admiration for Dietrich.

HJS This was something that was very important in her life: the adoration, if not idolization, that she received from gay people throughout the world.

PP Yes, she was very moved by this, and it made her very happy. She herself had numerous affairs with women, as is common knowledge. She enjoyed sexual ambiguity.

HJS In her first Hollywood film, she kisses an unknown woman full on the mouth in the Mogador cabaret, while the legionnaire Gary Cooper fans himself and blushes.

PP This was the kind of ambience she adored. It amazed and excited her to be recognized, loved, and imitated by people who displayed such courage. To be openly bisexual in the 1940s and 50s took guts, which Dietrich had in abundance. Her sense of honor and her courage galvanized her audiences, who recognized themselves in her struggles, her tolerance, and her unfettered freedom.

JOHN ENGSTEAD, 1939

Before Dietrich went to Universal's portrait gallery for the first time in 1939, she commissioned portraits from the Engstead-Higgins studio.

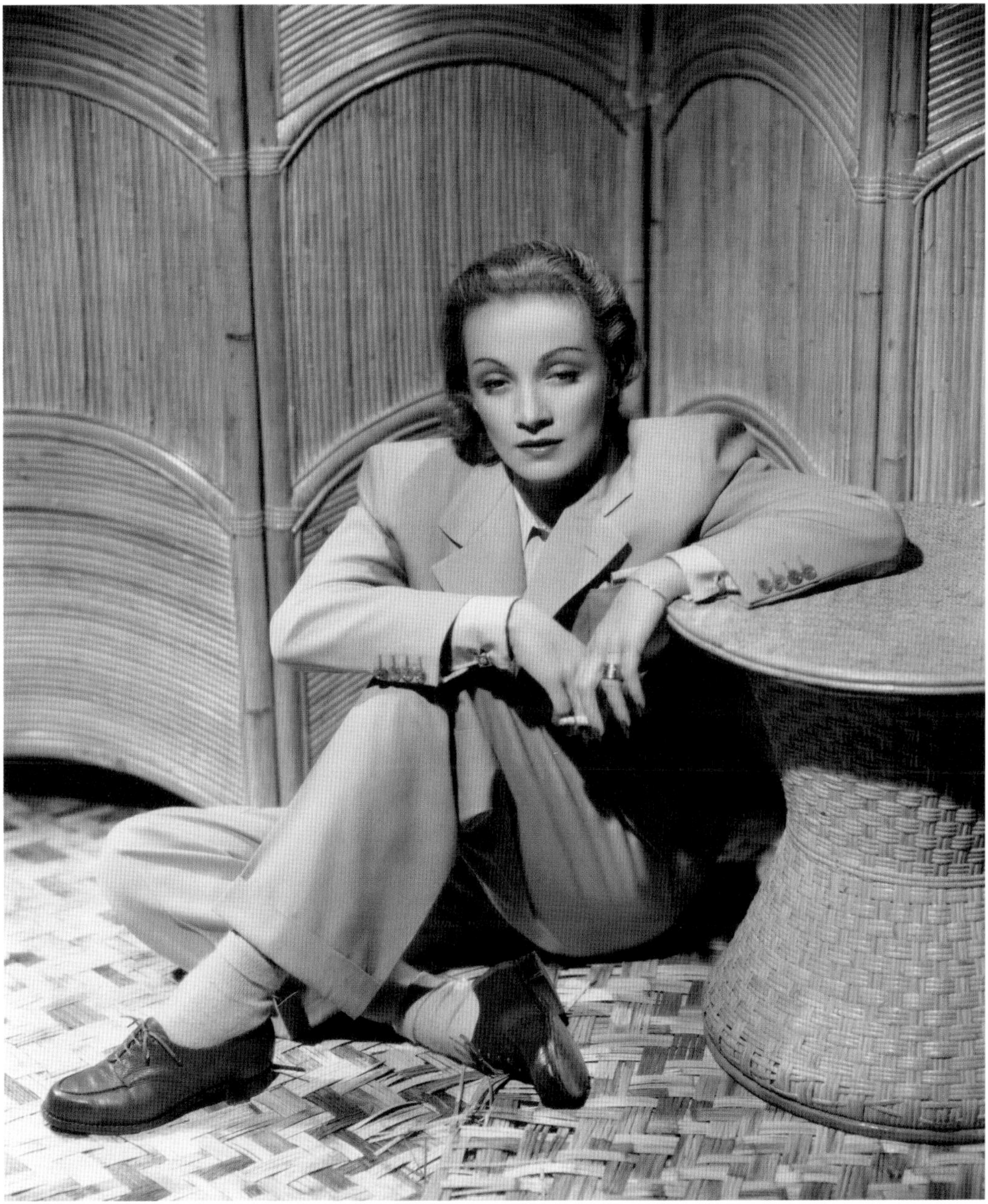

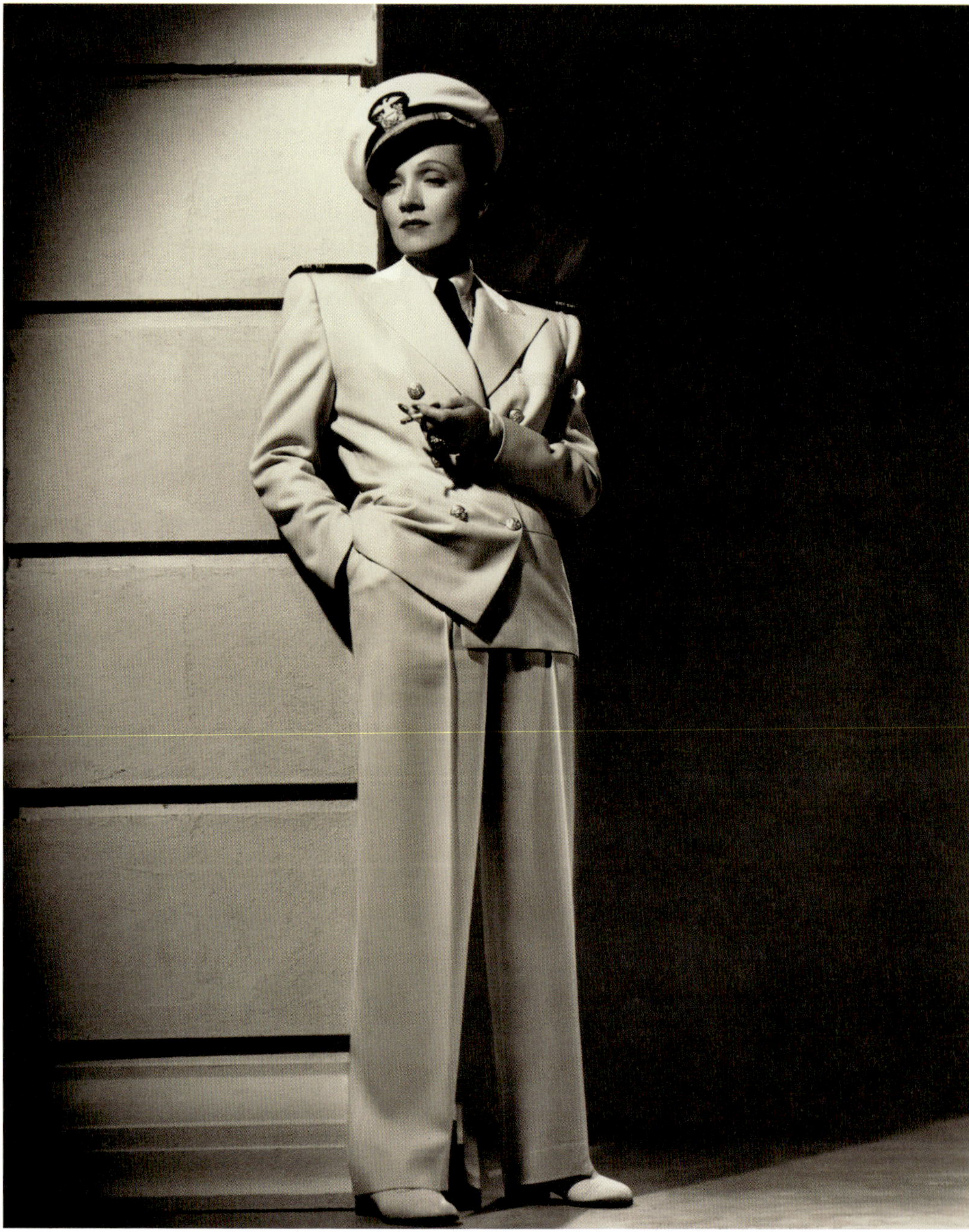

RAY JONES, 1940

By the time of Tay Garnett's *Seven Sinners*, audiences were amused, not scandalized, by Dietrich's cross dressing.

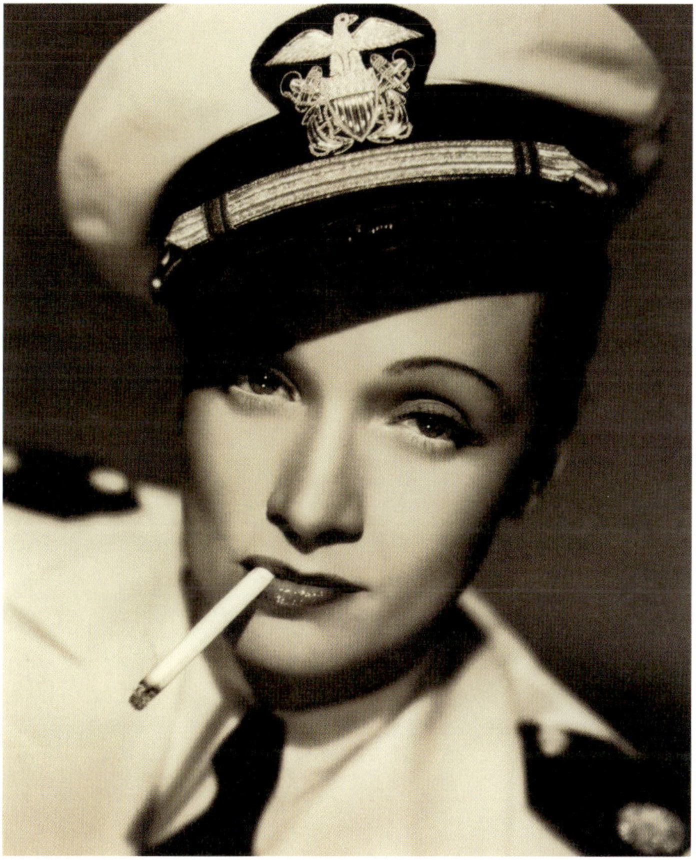

RAY JONES, 1940

This portrait was made for *Seven Sinners*. Jones's work could be bland and mechanical, but Dietrich helped him infuse it with drama and contrast.

"Now, look: In this experience
you be Dietrich and
I'll be the photographer."

IRVING PENN QUOTED BY JAY FIELDEN
IN "REMEMBERING IRVING PENN: THE STRANGER BEHIND
THE CAMERA," *VOGUE*, NOVEMBER 2004.

IRVING PENN, 1948

In 1948 the *Vogue* photographer Penn embarked on his celebrated "corner series," putting his subjects in the contained space between two flats. This portrait was shot late that year.

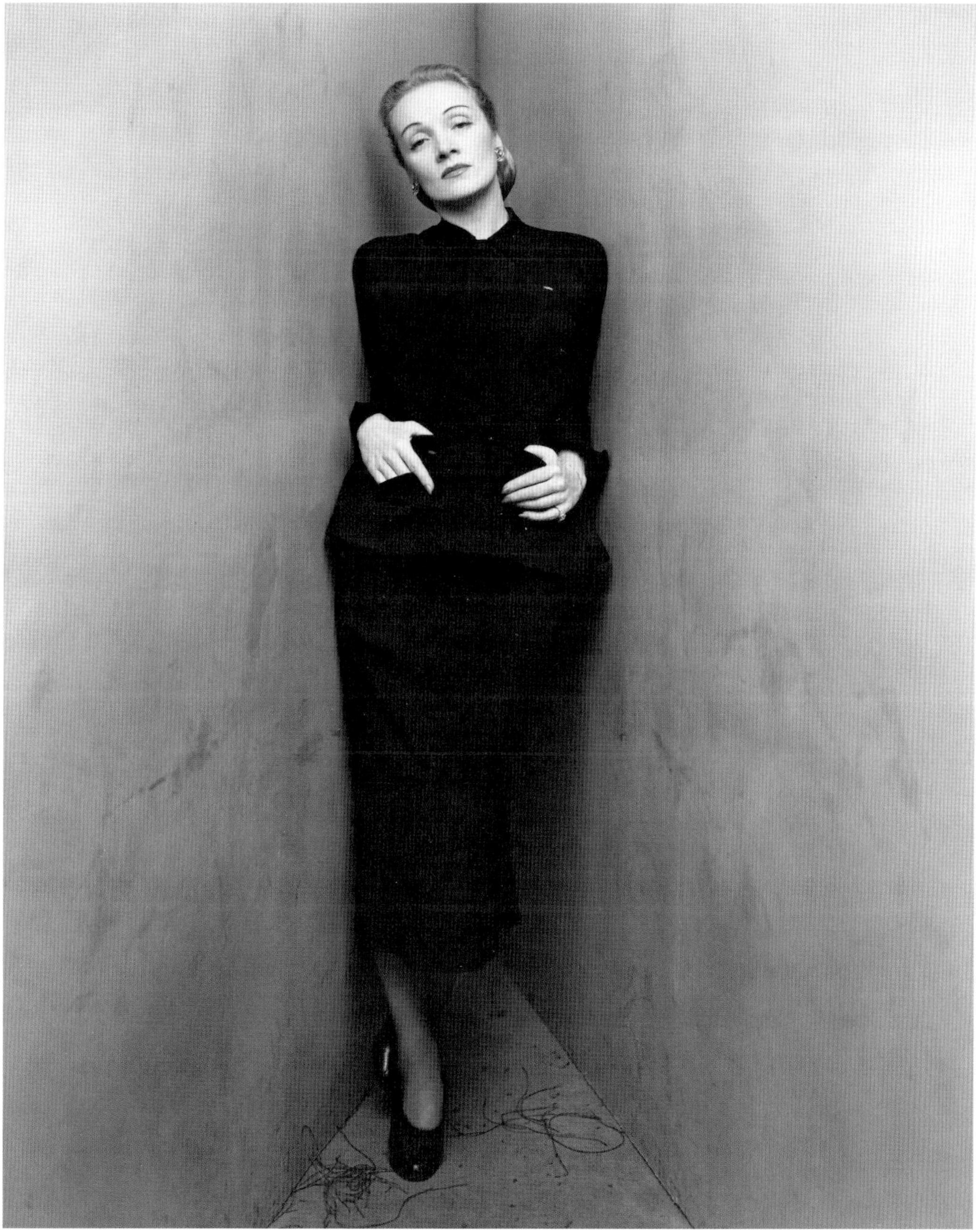

HJS Just as she herself was galvanized by her work against the Nazis.

PP That took a great deal of courage, especially as she was herself German. In 1942, not many people in Germany knew of the existence of concentration camps, nor what went on in them. Dietrich had foreseen the catastrophe that unfolded. She was decorated for her service by France, the United States, and Israel: in 1947, she was awarded the Medal of Freedom, America's highest civilian distinction; in 1949 she was made a Chevalier of the Légion d'Honneur in France, raised to the rank of Officer in 1971 and Commander in 1989; and in 1965 she was awarded the Israeli Medal of Valor.

HJS She had a "homemaker" side, she loved to cook for her man. In the room she shared with Jean Gabin at the Hôtel Plaza Athénée—her first address in Paris before she moved into the Hotel Lancaster, where she lived for many years and where the lilac suite she occupied has been restored as it was then—she would concoct many a delicious pot-au-feu for Gabin, while at the same time unleashing impassioned diatribes against the Nazi regime. These two occupations sum her up quite neatly.

PP Her commitment to war work against the Nazis lends her a tragic dimension, a transcendent quality. She showed enormous courage in her political opposition to the Third Reich. In an article published in *Welcome* before the war, she declared, "I am German, I know the Germans. We are a very obedient people, and if we start to obey someone like Herr Hitler that becomes very dangerous." She had a sense of the way things were going, an intuitive understanding that was incredible.

HJS That she, a German citizen, should have stood up against the ruling power in her own country with such eloquence and humanity compels our admiration, and makes her—once again—all the more human and endearing. And modern.

PP Something else that makes her so glamorous and modern is her tremendous sense of humor. Often at her own expense: "I've played so many courtesans that people think I'm a whore." She loved to laugh, to make other people laugh, and to poke fun at herself.

LASZLO WILLINGER, 1943

Dietrich took a break from entertaining the troops in World War II and made the exotic *Kismet* at MGM. As she arrived, the brilliant Willinger was leaving, so there was only time for one short session.

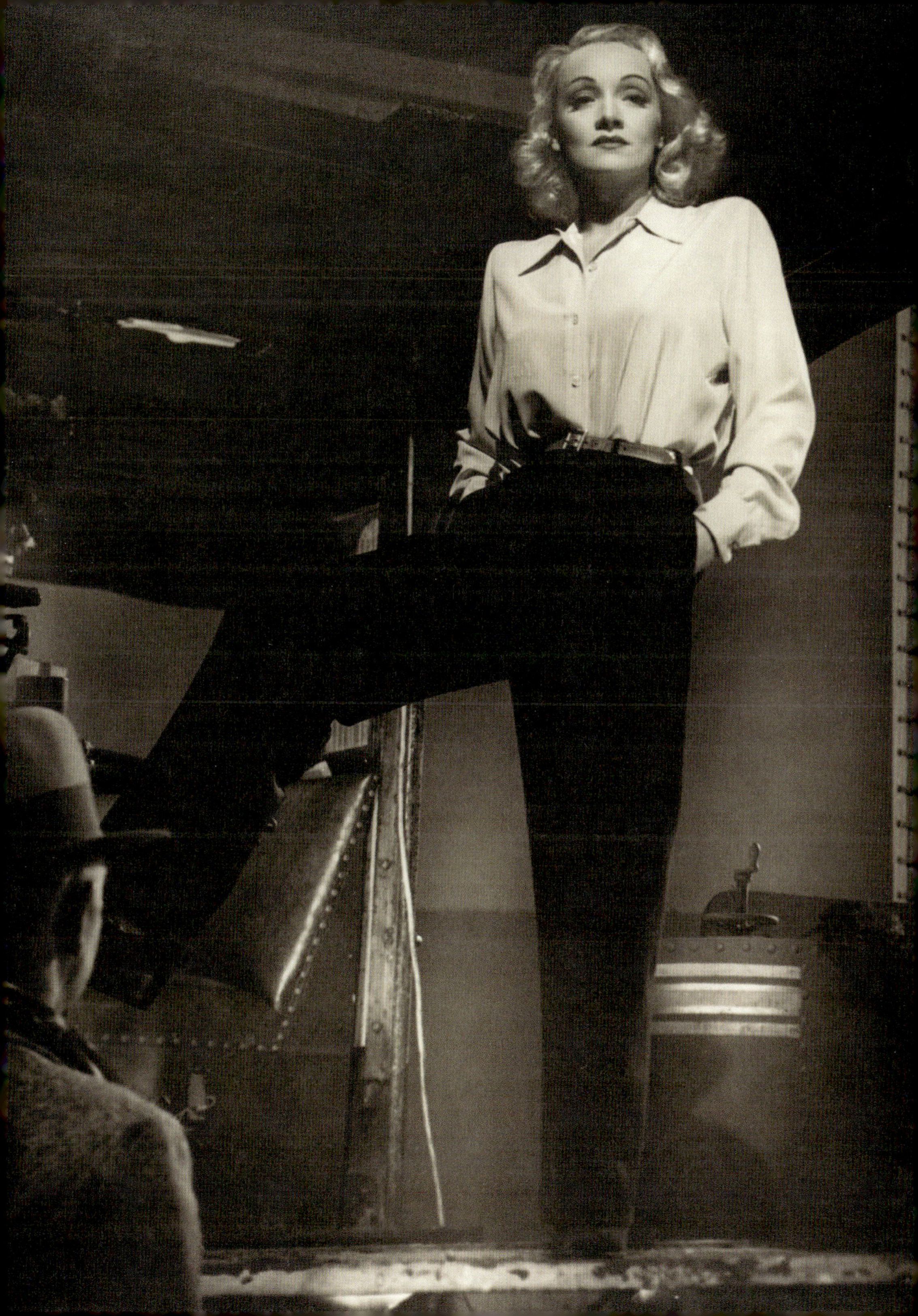

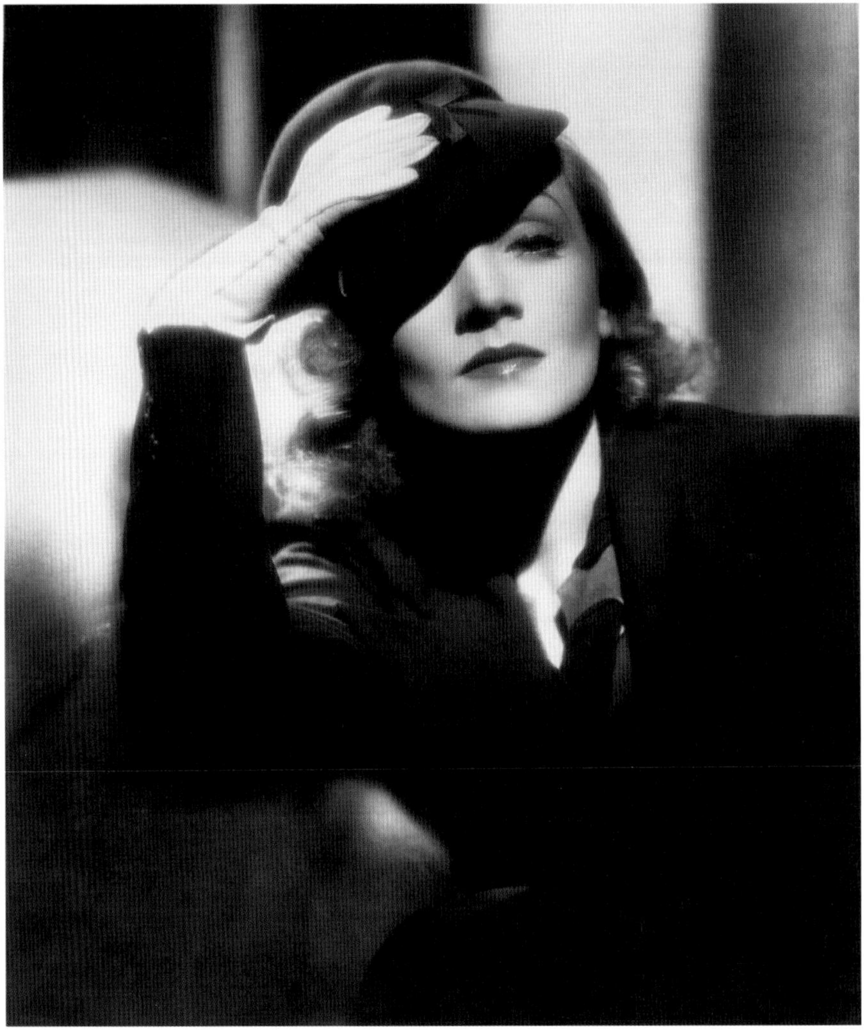

EUGENE ROBERT RICHEE, 1937

This portrait was part of a session made to publicize Ernst Lubitsch's *Angel*. When the film was amended to appease censors, it lost its box-office potential and hastened Dietrich's departure from Paramount.

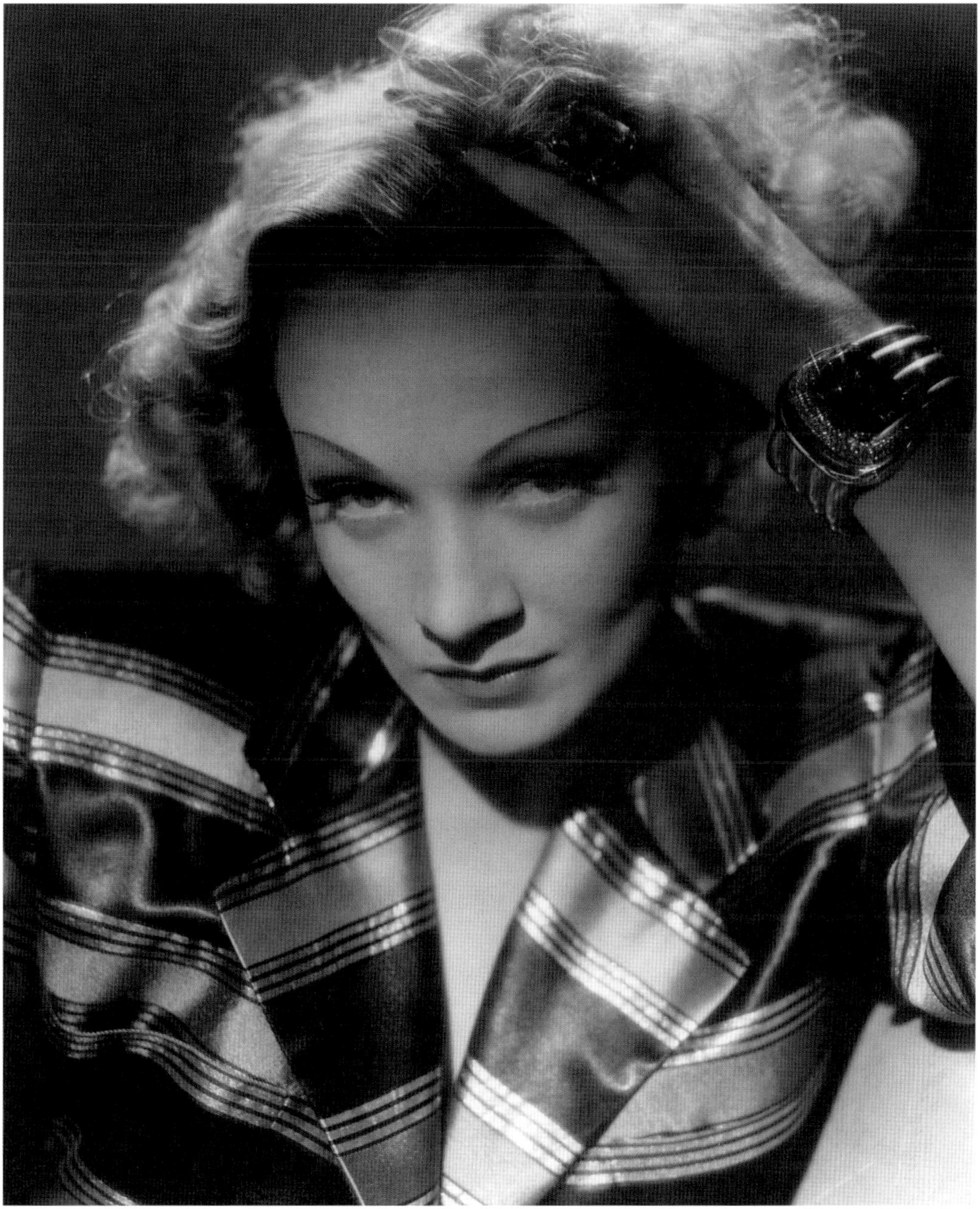

JOHN ENGSTEAD, 1940

Dietrich came to John Engstead when she learned that he had been forced out of his position as head of publicity at Paramount. He joined another photographer to open his own studio in Beverly Hills.

"The Perpetuation of 'Marlene Dietrich'—the legend and the artifact—was one of the most disciplined and sustained creative acts of the twentieth century."

STEVEN BACH, *MARLENE DIETRICH: LIFE AND LEGEND*, 1992.

JOHN ENGSTEAD, 1940

When Dietrich posed for Engstead in his Beverly Hills studio, he was also shooting fashion work for women's magazines.

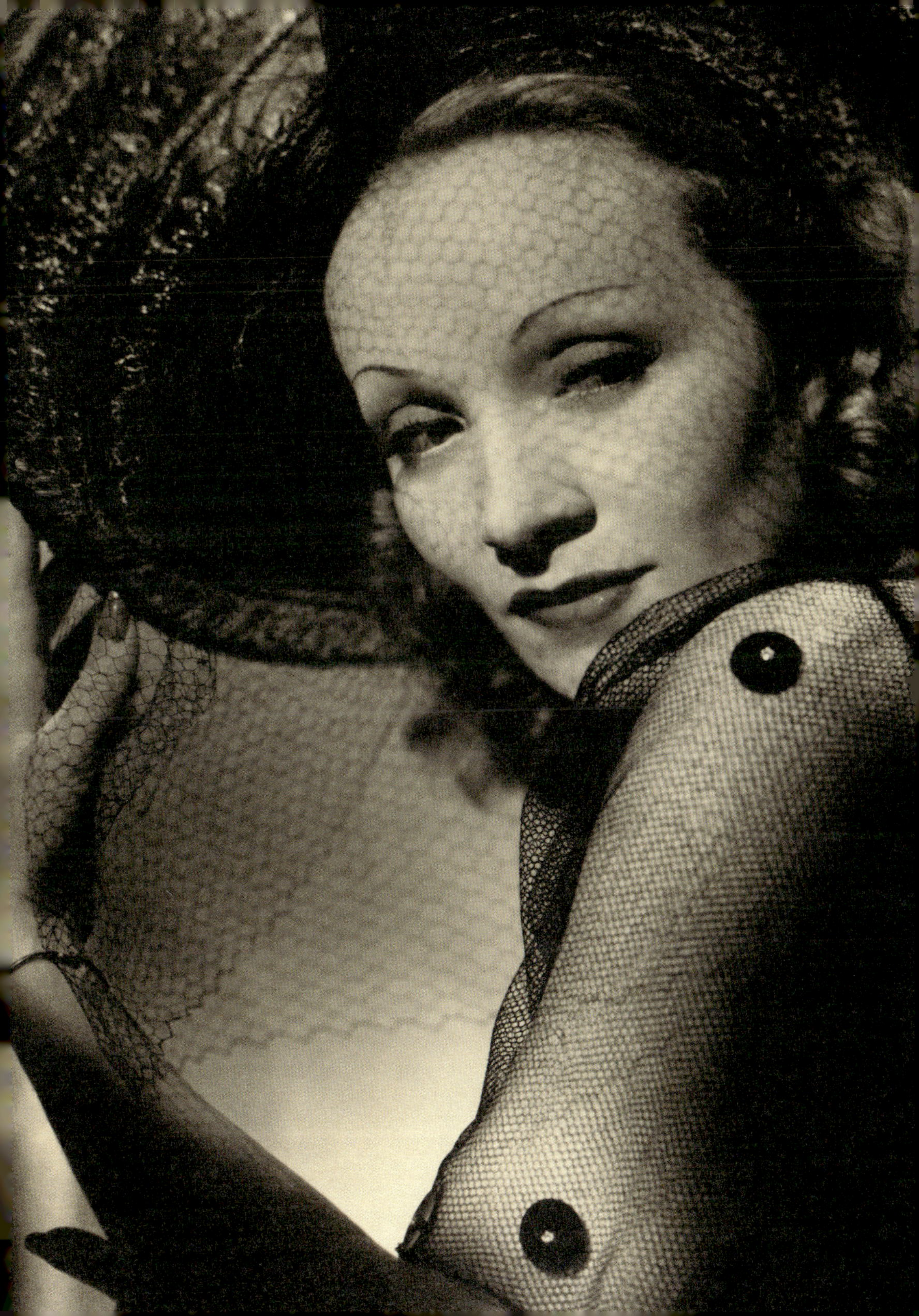

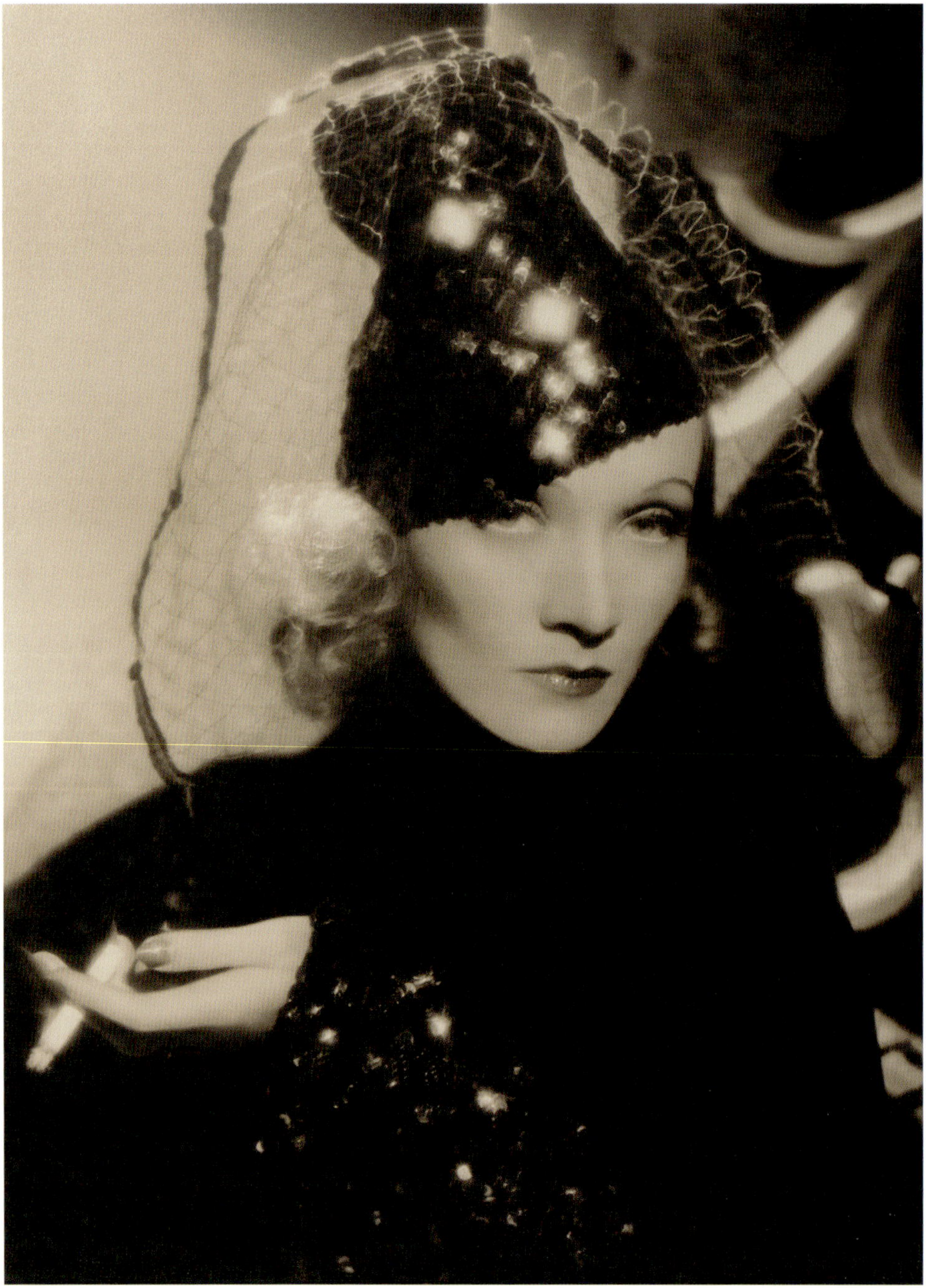

EUGENE ROBERT RICHEE, 1937

Dietrich's last Paramount portrait session was done with Richee, and many of the images betrayed the feeling that Dietrich's tenure had run its course.

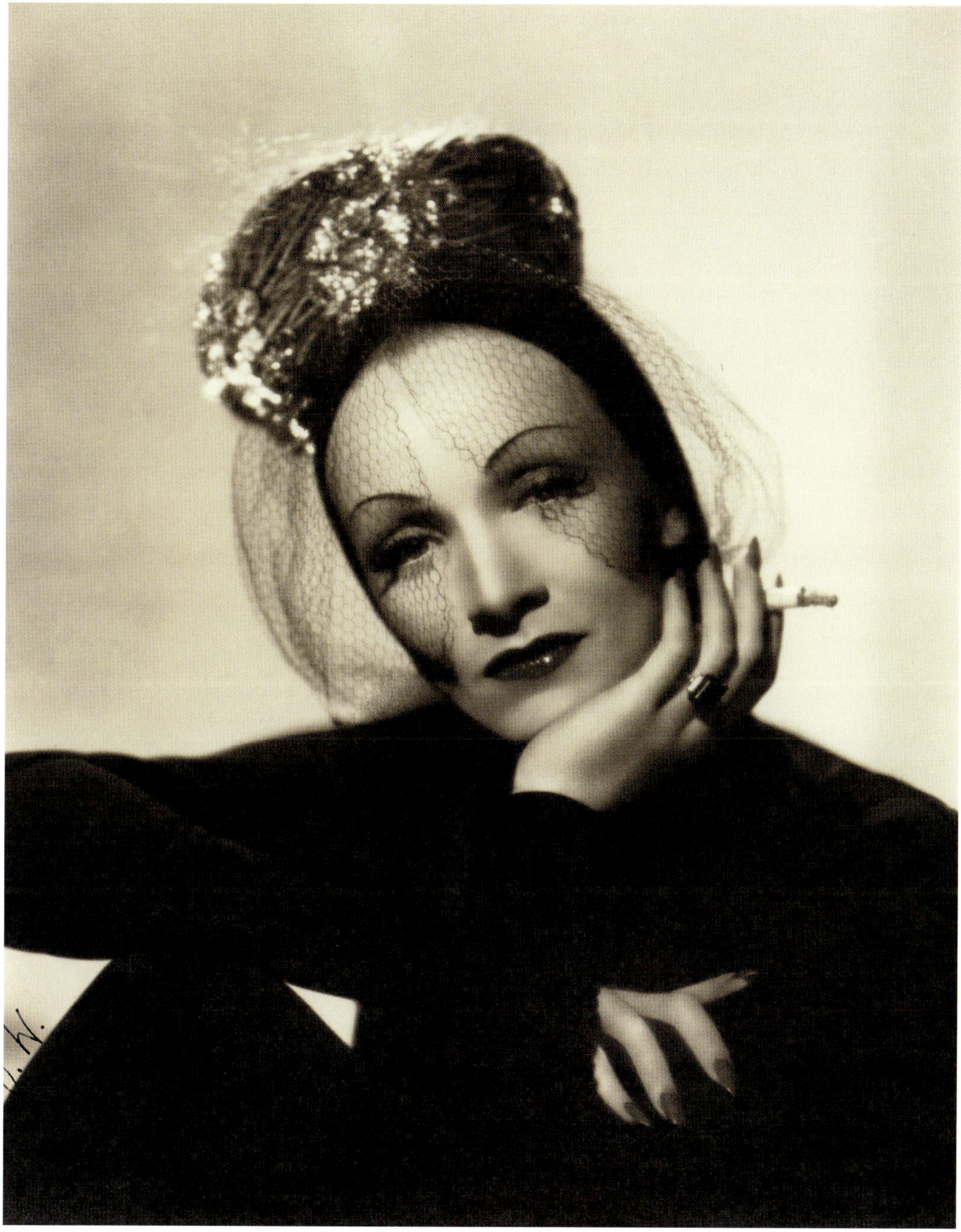

RAY JONES, 1940

The Universal publicity department needed fashion poses to send to magazines. Dietrich was happy to cooperate.

HJS Because she radiates beauty and a sense of freedom in her photographs, she manages to give the impression that she is part of the studio system but at the same time she is not a prisoner of it. She seems to glide above the world order.

PP She is the embodiment of a liberated woman. Even though she was married. Who knows who Dietrich's husband was? Who even knows that she was married to the same man her whole life? In fact, she was never dependent on any man. And on screen she gave the impression of never once obeying a man. Of never needing a man to guide her. The scenarios she played out were driven by one thing and one thing only: love. It was an obsession that shines through in so many of her photographs, that makes it so easy for us to love her today.

To end, I'd like to quote Jean Gabin (a passionate horse-enthusiast) after his break-up with Marlene: "That filly is impossible to drive."

Paris, September 2017

HORST P. HORST, 1947

Dietrich modeled Christian Dior's Chandernagore ensemble at Horst's New York studio for the December 1947 issue of *Vogue* magazine.

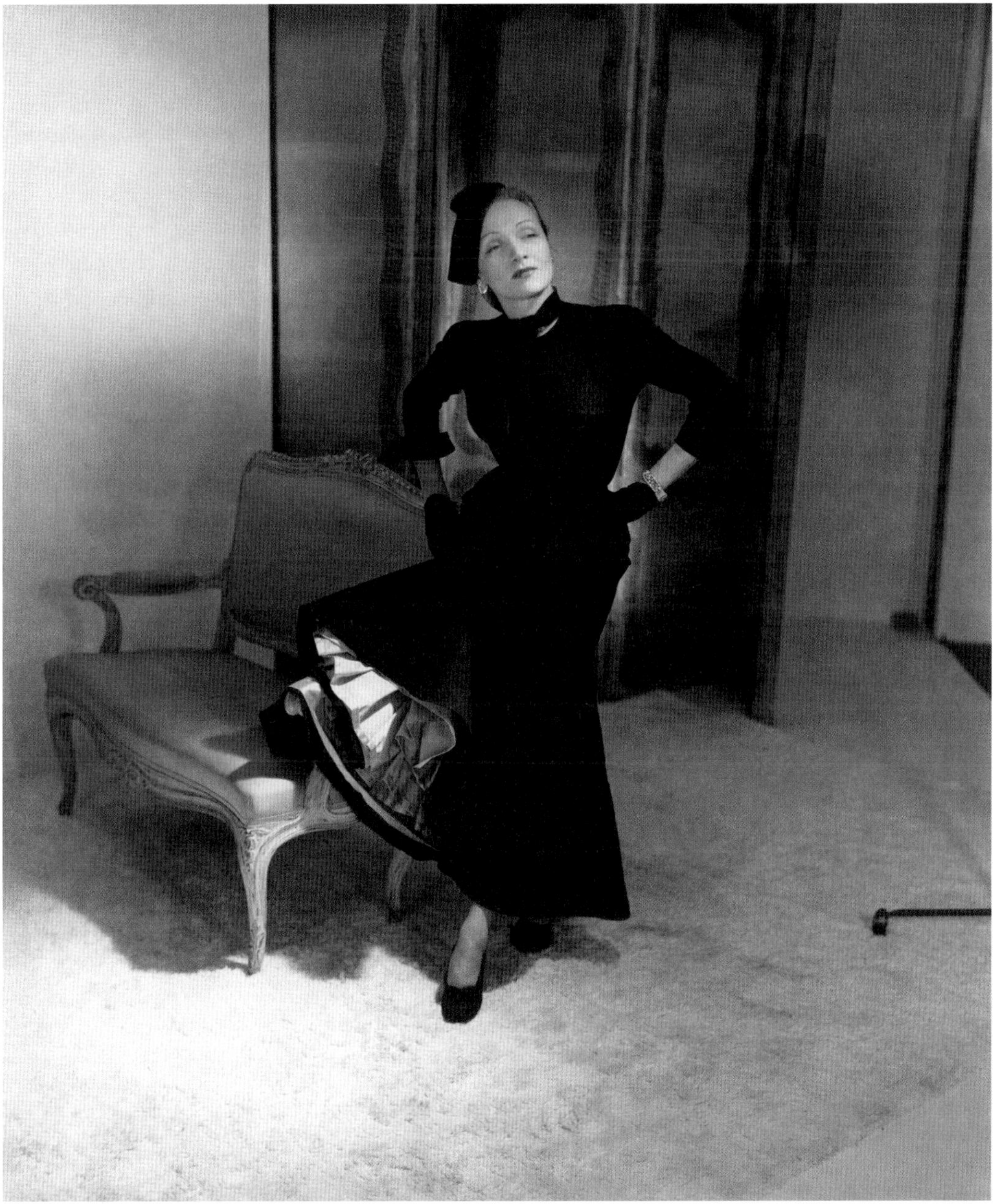

"Dietrich is frequently mentioned as an actress whose screen presence raises questions about women's representation in Hollywood cinema. She has also acquired her own cult following of male and female, straight and gay admirers."

GAYLYN STUDLAR, *IN THE REALM OF PLEASURE*, 1988.

MILTON H. GREENE, 1952

This portrait by photographer-producer Milton Greene ran in the August 18, 1952 issue of *Life* magazine. It illustrated an in-depth article on Dietrich's life and career.

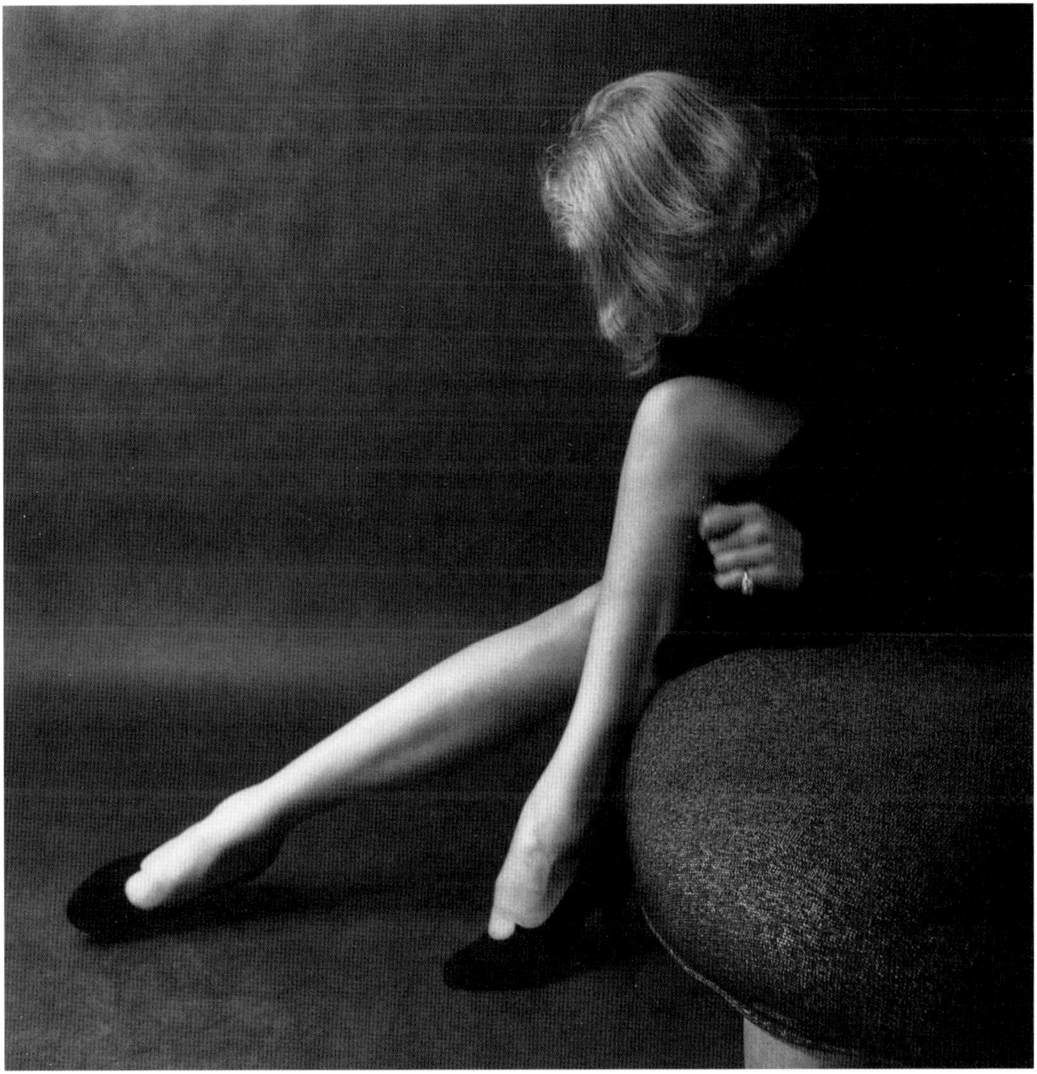

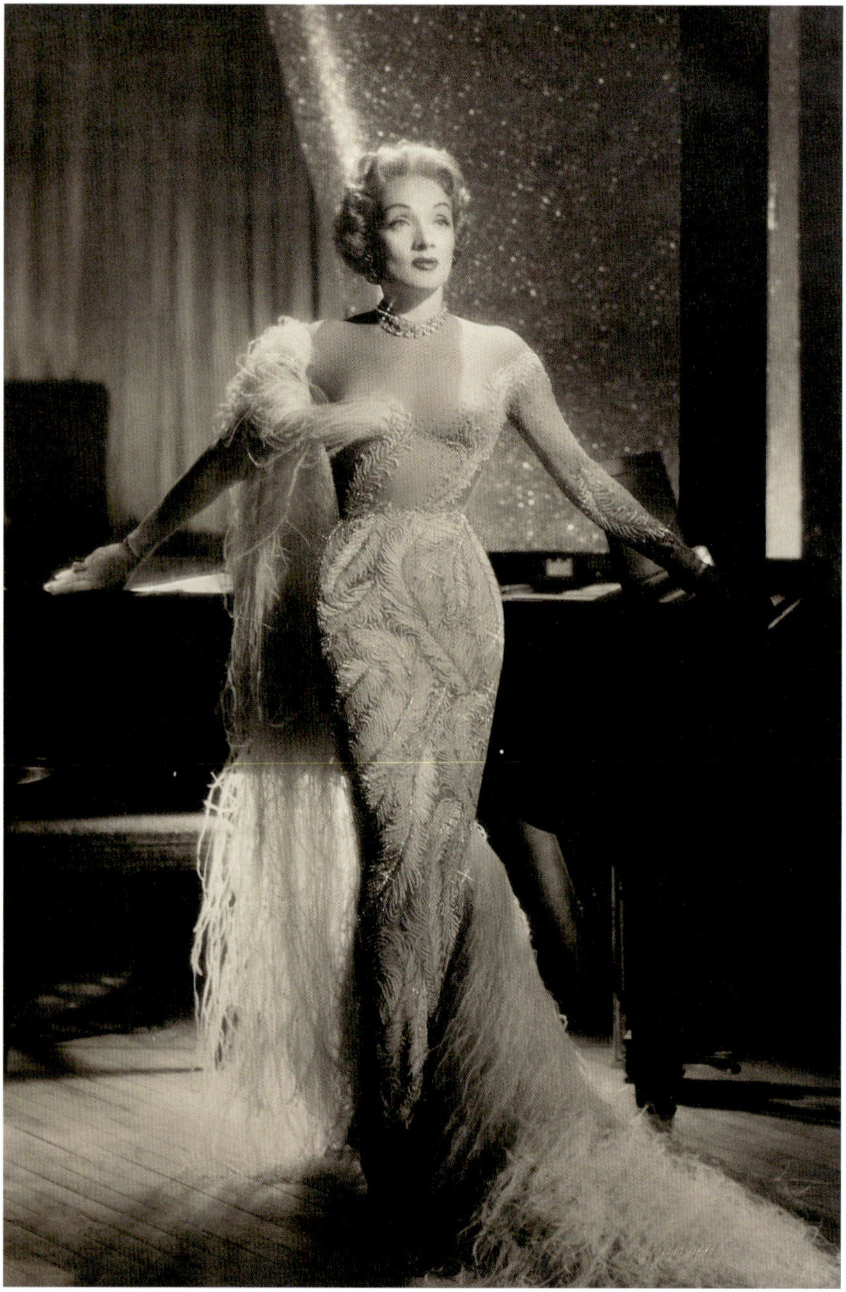

JOHN ENGSTEAD, 1955

Dietrich conquered Las Vegas with a dazzling show and a translucent gown designed by Jean Louis. For publicity portraits she turned to Engstead, who had built a studio in West Hollywood.

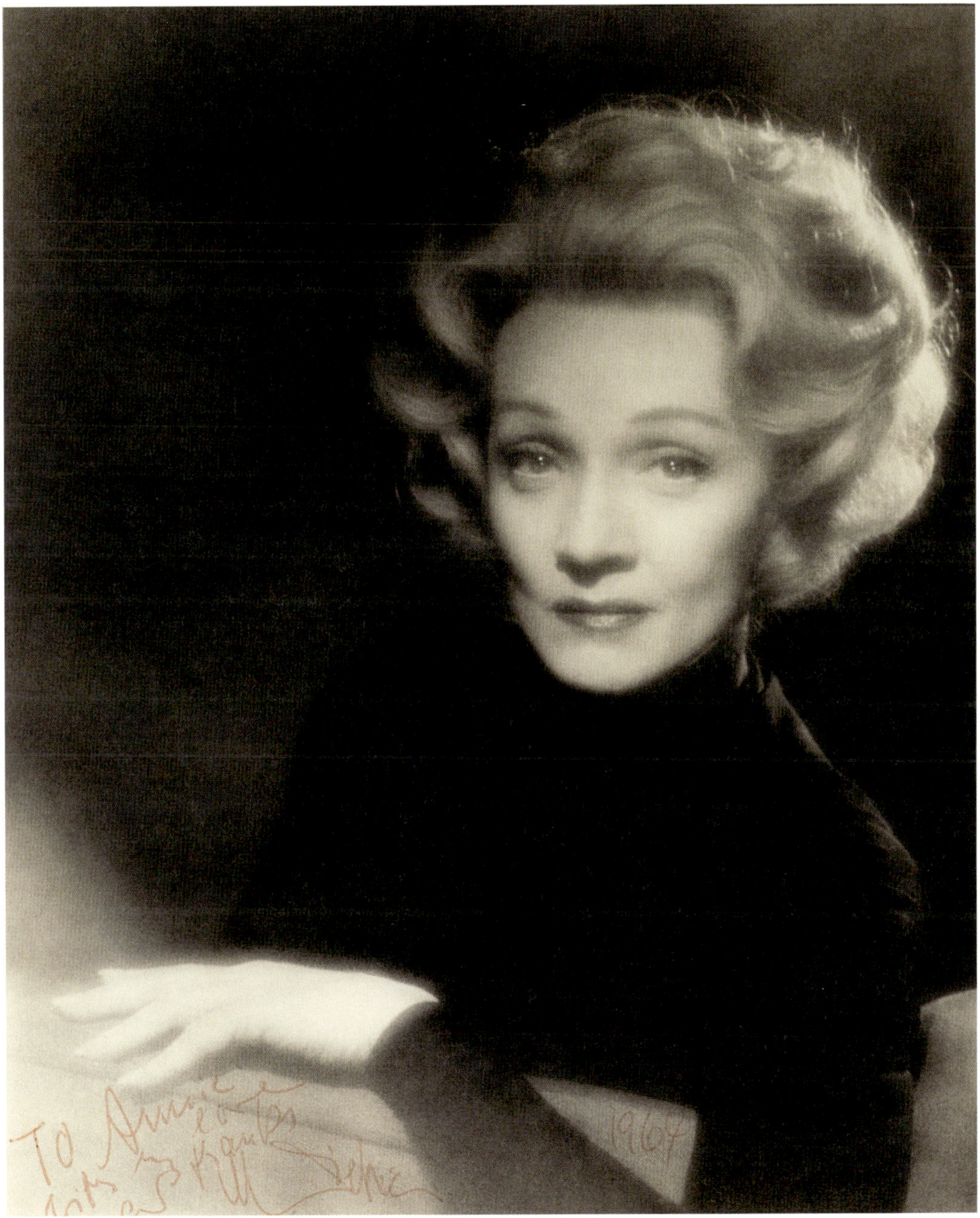

UNSIGNED PHOTOGRAPH FOR CAPITOL RECORDS PHOTO, 1967

One of Dietrich's best-selling albums was a three-disc set featuring standards performed in her concerts.

"The name Marlene Dietrich, more than any other, blends with the essence of cinema. A number of actresses become stars, some of them become myths."

JACQUES CHIRAC

WILLY RIZZO, 1956

In 1956, Dietrich posed for the Italian photographer Rizzo in Cannes, showing that her legs were still sensational. By this time she was known as "the world's most glamorous grandmother," an epithet she detested. (Willy Rizzo © Paris Match/Scoop archives.)

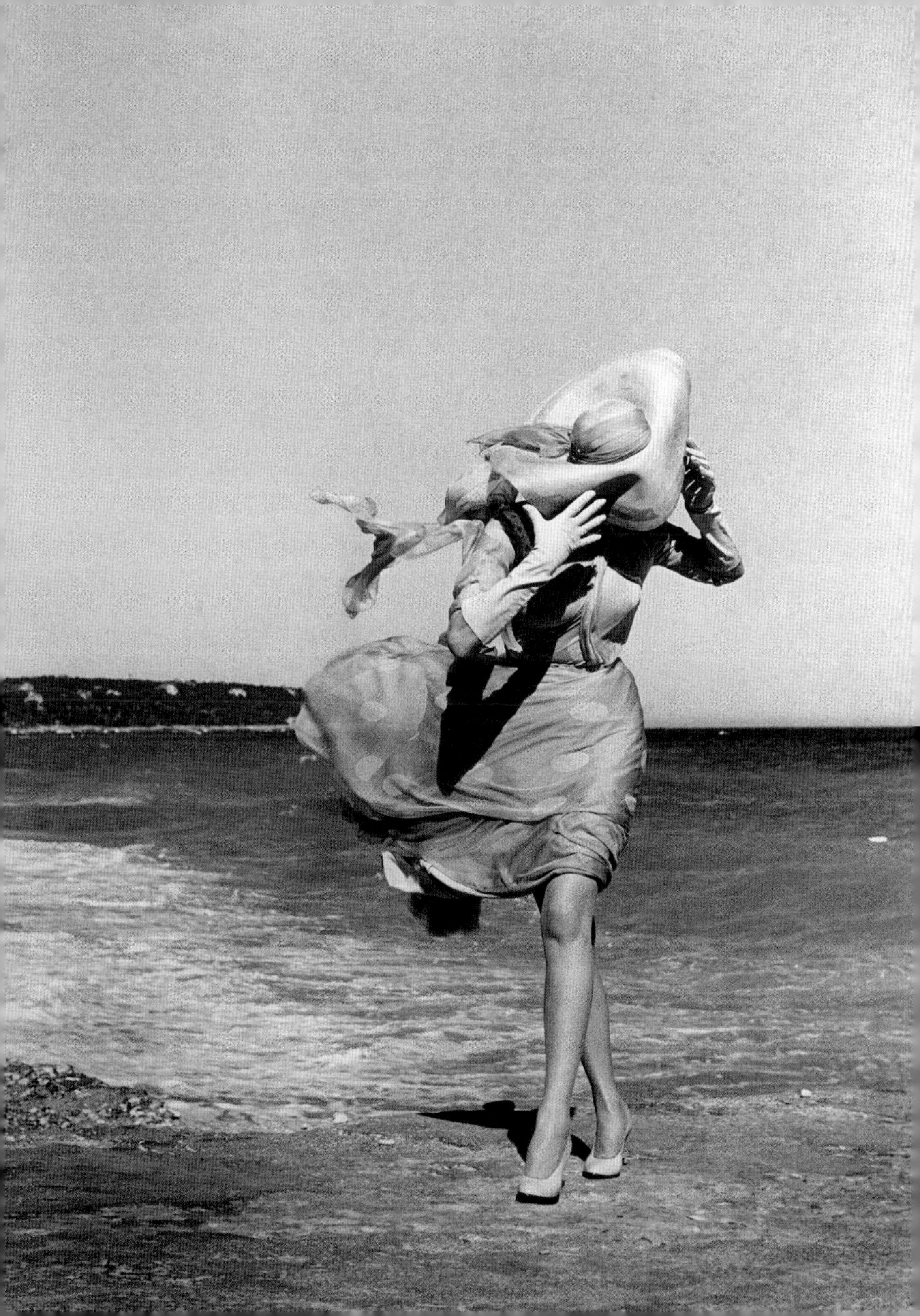

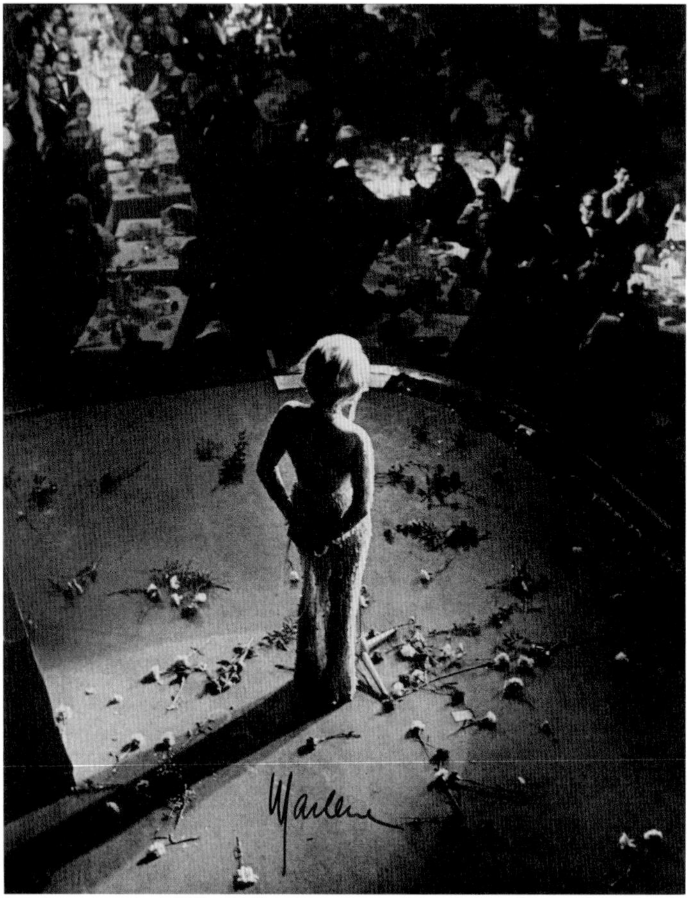

BENGT H. MALMQVIST, 1963

The Swedish photographer known for his portraits of musicians and performers took this photo at a 1963 concert in Stockholm.

FRANÇOIS GRAGNON, 1959

In 1959, Dietrich gave a show in the Théâtre de l'Étoile, Paris, wearing an outfit by Jean Louis.

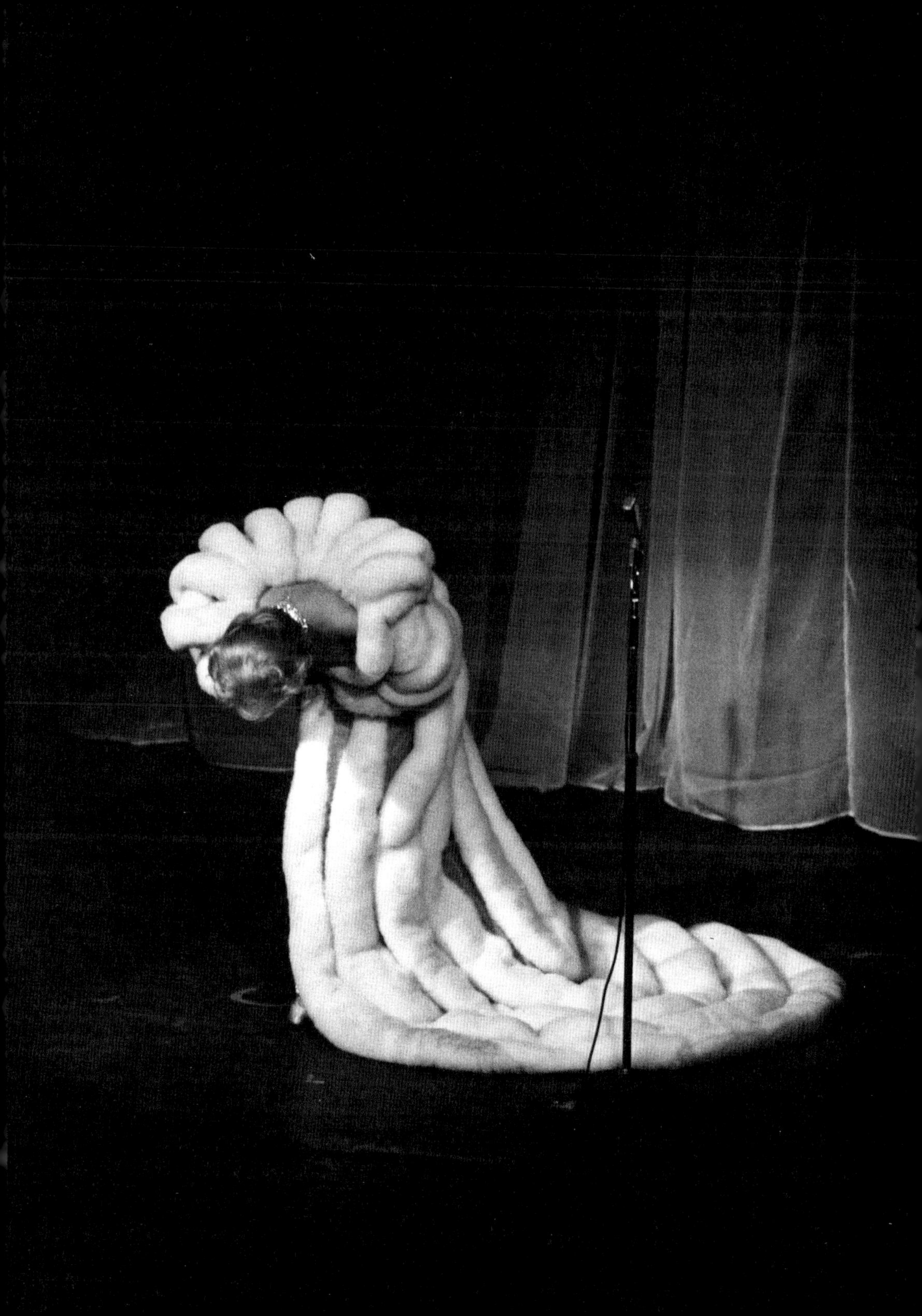

PIERRE PASSEBON
Creator of the Galerie du Passage, Pierre Passebon is a French gallery owner and collector. With 2000 works, he owns one of the most complete photograph collections dedicated to Marlene Dietrich.

HENRY-JEAN SERVAT
Henri-Jean Servat has extensively written for *Midi Libre, Libération,* and *Paris Match*. He participates to numerous French TV shows and he published *Brigitte Bardot: My Life in Fashion* (Flammarion, 2016).

AKNOWLEDGMENTS
Pierre Passebon would like to express his sincere gratitude to Judith Benhamou-Huet, Patrice Calmettes, Jean-Luc Monterosso, and Henry-Jean Servat.

Cover
SCOTTY WELBOURNE, 1941

After Dietrich made a film called *Manpower* at Warner Bros., she posed for publicity portraits, instructing Welbourne how to properly position the light to achieve her trademark look.